KU-051-588

COLLINS GEM

READY REFERENCE

Trevor Bounford
with
The Diagram Group

HarperCollins*Publishers*

HarperCollins Publishers
P.O. Box, Glasgow G4 0NB

A Diagram Book first created by Diagram Visual
Information Limited of 195 Kentish Town Road,
London NW5 8SY, England

First published 1992
© Diagram Visual Information Limited 1992
Reprint 10 9 8 7 6 5 4 3 2 1 0

ISBN 0 00 458974 2
All rights reserved

Printed in Great Britain by
HarperCollins Manufacturing, Glasgow

Foreword

Measurements are used to help establish the size of something. How far is it to the Moon? What is the page size of this book? How strong is the wind? So that these questions may be answered, many standards of measurement have been developed, encompassing things as diverse as radio wavelengths, wind speeds, earthquakes and laundry codes. Different standards have been created around the world, and units based on both the imperial and metric systems of measurement are now encountered. As a result, knowledge is needed of how to convert values from one system to another. The simple need to measure has created a complex web of units that now affects every aspect of life.

The *Collins Gem Ready Reference* is a uniquely useful guide to this world of measures. The book is divided into twelve sections, each providing essential information on the main units of measurement or features of a particular topic. Where relevant, individual sections have conversion formulas, e.g. for metric and imperial conversion equivalents, with conversion tables to provide immediate visual reference.

The *Collins Gem Ready Reference* is an indispensable, handy-sized guide to the international variety in units of measurement. It is an essential companion, whether for school, office or home.

Contents

CONTENTS

5

How to use this book

The *Collins Gem Ready Reference* is divided into 12
sections, each of which is devoted to a particular
category of facts and figures. If you know which
category you wish to explore, merely turn to the table
of contents to find the relevant page number.

Unit conversion index

In this book, there are tables for converting units from
the imperial system of measurement to the metric
system (and vice versa), and for converting one type of
unit to another within the same system. The Unit
Conversion Index enables you to refer quickly to the
tables in which a particular unit is converted.

Formulas

Within each section, you will find a selection of conversion formulas. These are easy-to-use formulas for
common conversions; you will need to use a calculator
for most of them, although many are simple, approximate conversions.

Conversion tables

Each group of units has its conversion tables: pages of
quick-reference tables for all imperial and metric
measurements from metres to feet, grains to grams.
These are particularly handy if you do not have a
calculator. It would be impossible to accommodate
tables listing every possible conversion, and so the
material included is not exhaustive.

You can use the following to convert figures larger
than those in the table:

(a) separate the total into its parts: e.g., to convert 1536 units of something, first convert the largest part in the table (1000) and then each next largest part (500, 30, and 6). Then add these separate conversions together to find the total conversion; or

(b) move the decimal point in your original figure until the number is in the same form as those in the table. Look for the nearest number to this in the table and record the appropriate conversion. Then move the decimal point the same number of places in the oppsite direction to give an approximate conversion of your original number.

Note also that, because of lack of space, the figures in the conversion tables are rounded up or down to the third decimal place, and so are not always exact.

Unit conversion index

Glossary

acre A measure of land: originally the amount of land that a yoke of oxen could plough in a day. Equal to 4840 yd^2.

amu *see* Atomic mass unit.

ampere (A) The unit for measuring electric current.

ångström (Å) A unit of length, used mainly to measure the wavelength of light. Named after the Swedish physicist A.J. Ångström (1814–74). Equal to 10^{-10} m (10^{-8} cm).

apothecaries' system A system of weights used especially by pharmacists.

are (a) A unit of measure equal to an area of 10 x 10 m (1 a = 100 m^2). *See also* Hectare (ha): 100 a = 1 ha.

astronomical unit (au or AU) A unit of measure based on the distance between the Earth and the Sun. Approximately equal to 1.5 x 10^8 km.

atomic mass unit (amu)

    chemical A unit of mass equal to $1/16$ of the weighted mass of the three naturally occurring neutral oxygen isotopes.
    1 amu chemical = (1.660 ± 0.000 05) x 10^{-27} kg. Formerly called the atomic weight unit.

    international A unit of mass equal to $1/12$ of the mass of a neutral carbon-12 atom. 1 amu international = (1.660 33 ± 0.000 05) x 10^{-27} kg.

    physical A unit of mass equal to $1/16$ of the mass of an oxygen atom. 1 amu physical = 1.660 x 10^{-27} kg.

atto- In the UK, a prefix meaning a trillionth (10^{-18}); in the US, meaning a quintillionth (10^{-18}). For example, in

the UK 1 attometre = 1 trillionth of a metre; in the US,
1 attometre = 1 quintillionth of a metre.

avoirdupois system A system of weights based on the
16-oz pound and the 16-dram ounce.

baker's dozen A counting unit equal to 13.

barleycorn A unit of measure of length equal to ⅓ in.

billion (bil) In the UK, equal to 10^{12}; in US, equal to
10^9. Commonly now also used in the UK to mean 10^9.

bolt A measure of length, usually for fabric. In the UK,
a bolt of cloth equals 42 yd; in the US, a bolt of
wallpaper equals 16 yd and a bolt of cloth equals 40 yd.

British thermal unit (Btu) Measure of heat needed to
raise the temperature of one pound of water by 1 °F.
Equal to 252 calories.

bushel (bu) A measure of dry volume. In the UK, 1 bu
= 8 gal (64 UK pt); in the US, 1 bu = 8 gal (64 US pt).
The measures are not to be confused: 1 UK bu = 1.03
US bu.

calibre A unit of length used to measure the diameter of
a tube or the bore of a firearm, in ¹⁄₁₀₀ in or ¹⁄₁₀₀₀ in
increments.

calorie (cal) A measure of heat energy representing the
amount of heat needed to raise 1 g of water by 1 °C.
Also called 'small calorie': 1000 cal = 1 kcal or Cal.
See also Joule; Kilocalorie.

carat A unit of weight equal to 200 mg (3.1 grains).
Also used as a measure of gold purity (per 24 parts gold
alloy).

centi- Prefix meaning a hundred or ¹⁄₁₀₀; e.g., a centilitre
(cl) is a unit of volume equal to ¹⁄₁₀₀ (0.01) litre.

centrad A measure of a plane angle, especially used to measure the angular deviation of light through a prism. 1 centrad = $\frac{1}{100}$ (0.01) radian.

century A measure of time equal to 100 years.

chain A measure of length equal to 22 yd. Also known as Gunter's chain.

> **engineer's chain** A measure of length equal to 100 ft.
>
> **nautical chain** A measure of length equal to 15 ft.
>
> **square chain** A measure of area equal to 484 yd^2.

chaldron A measure of volume. In the UK, 1 chaldron = 36 UK bu (288 gal); in the US, 1 chaldron = 36 US bu.

cord A unit of dry volume, especially used for timber. Equal to 128 ft^3.

cubic units (cu or ^{3}) These are arrived at by multiplying a number by itself twice. With a three dimensional object, the height, breadth and length are multiplied togther to give its volume, which is measured in cubic units.

cubit A unit of length approximately equal to 18 in. Originally based on the distance from tip of middle finger to elbow.

cup A measure of volume (either liquid or solid) used especially in cooking. In the UK, 1 cup = ½ UK pt (16 tbsp); in the US, 1 cup = ½ US pt (16 tbsp). The two should not be confused: 1 UK cup = 1⅕ US cup.

day

> **mean solar day** A measure of time representing the interval between consecutive passages of the Sun across the meridian, averaged over 1 year.

1 day = 24 hr (86 400 s).

sidereal day A measure of time equal to approximately 23 hr, 56 min, 4.09 s. A sidereal day represents the time needed for one complete rotation of the Earth on its axis.

deca- Prefix meaning ten; e.g., a decametre is a measure of length equal to 10 m.

decade A measure of time equal to 10 years.

deci- Prefix meaning $\frac{1}{10}$; e.g., a decilitre (dl) is a measure of liquid volume equalling $\frac{1}{10}$ (0.01) litre.

decibel (dB) A measure of relative sound intensity.

degree (°)

    geometrical A unit of measure of plane angle equal to $\frac{1}{360}$ of the circumference of a circle (1 circle = 360°).

    temperature A measure of temperature difference representing a single division on the temperature scale. The centigrade scale has 100 equal degrees; the Fahrenheit scale has 180 equal degrees.

digit One of ten Arabic symbols representing numbers 0 to 9. Also used in astronomy as a unit of measure equal to $\frac{1}{12}$ the diameter of the Sun or Moon. Used in ancient Egypt as a measure of length: 1 digit = 1 finger width.

douzieme A unit of length equal to $\frac{1}{12}$ line.

dozen A counting unit equal to 12 times the original unit.

drachm A unit of mass in the apothecaries' system. 1 drachm = $\frac{1}{8}$ apothecaries' ounce (60 grains).

dram (dr) A unit of mass equal to $\frac{1}{16}$ oz.

    fluid dram A unit of liquid volume. In the UK, 1 dr = $\frac{1}{8}$ UK fl oz; in the US, 1 dr = $\frac{1}{8}$ US fl oz. The two should not be confused:

1 UK fl dr = 0.960 759 US fl dr.

dry Used in US to distinguish measure of dry (solid) volume as opposed to liquid (fluid) volume. For example, in the UK, the pint measures both dry and liquid volume. In the US, 1 fl pt = ⅛ US gal; 1 dry pt = ¹⁄₆₄ US bu. 1 US dry pt ≈ 0.969 UK pt ≈ 1.163 US fl pt.

dyne A unit of force equal to that needed to produce acceleration of 1 cm per second in a mass of 1 g. Replaced by the newton (N): 1 dyne = 10^{-5} N.

electronvolt (eV) A unit of energy measurement representing the energy acquired by an electron in passing through a potential difference of 1 volt. 1 eV = $(1.6 \pm 0.000\ 07) \times 10^{-19}$ J.

erg A unit of energy measurement equal to the energy produced by a force of one dyne through a distance of 1 cm. Replaced by the joule, 1 erg = 10^{-7} J.

fathom (fm) Unit of length, especially used to measure marine depth. 1 fm = 6 ft. Originally based on the span of two outstretched arms.

feet per minute A unit of velocity representing the number of feet travelled in 1 min.

femto- In the UK, a prefix meaning 1 thousand billionth (10^{-15}); in the US, meaning 1 quadrillionth (10^{-15}).

firkin A unit of volume, used especially to measure beer or ale. In the UK, 1 firkin = 9 UK gal; in the US, 1 firkin = 9.8 US gal.

fluid Used to distinguish units of liquid (fluid) volume as opposed to dry (solid) volume.

fluid dram *see* Dram.

fluid ounce *see* Ounce.

foot (ft) A unit of length equal to 12 in.

furlong (fur) Unit of length equal to ⅛ mi (660 ft).

gallon (gal) A unit of liquid volume. In the UK, 1 gal = 8 UK pt; in the US, 1 gal = 8 US pt. The two should not be confused: 1 UK gal = 1.2 US gal.

> **Winchester wine gallon (WWG)** A unit of volume used for wine, honey, or other liquids. Equal to 0.83 UK gal.

gauge A unit of length used to measure the diameter of a shotgun bore; e.g., 6-gauge equals 23.34 mm. Originally based on the number of balls, of certain size, contained in 1 lb.

giga- In the UK, a prefix meaning 1 thousand million (10^9); in the US, meaning 1 billion (10^9). For example, in the UK, 1 gigametre = 1 thousand million metres; in the US, 1 gigametre = 1 billion metres.

gill A unit of liquid volume. In the UK, 1 gill = ¼ UK pt; in US (gi), 1 gi = ¼ US fl pt. The two should not be confused: 1 UK gill = ½ US gi.

grade (g) A measure of plane angle in geometry. $1^{\text{g}} = 0.9°$.

grain (gr) A unit of mass measurement, used especially in the apothecaries' system. 1 grain = ⅟₇₀₀₀ lb (avoirdupois); 480 grains = 1 ounce troy; 24 grains = 1 pennyweight.

gram (g) A unit of mass or volume measurement. 1 g = 0.001 kg.

gross A counting measure equal to 144 (or 12 dozen) of the original unit.

hand A unit of length, used especially to measure horses' height. 1 hand = 4 in.

hectare (ha) A measure of area, usually of land, equal to 10 000 m².

hecto- Prefix meaning 100; e.g., a hectometre (hm) is a unit of length equal to 100 m.

hertz (Hz) A unit of frequency measurement equal to 1 cycle per second.

horsepower (hp) A unit of work representing the power needed to raise 550 lb by 1 ft in 1 s.

   metric horsepower A unit of power representing that needed to raise a 75-kg mass 1 m in 1 s.

hour (hr) A unit of time measurement equal to 60 min (3600 s).

hundredweight (cwt) A unit of mass.

   1 hundredweight =112 lb; 1 hundredweight troy = 100 pounds troy; 1 hundredweight = 4 quarters.

   short hundredweight (sh cwt) US name for the UK Quintal or Cental.

   1 short hundredweight = 100 lb.

inch (in) A unit of length equal to ¹⁄₂ ft.

inches per second A unit of velocity representing the number of inches travelled in 1 s.

joule (J) A unit of energy equal to the work done when a force of 1 newton is moved through a distance of 1 m. Used instead of calorie: 1 J = 0.239 cal. Named after J.P. Joule (1818–89).

keg A unit of volume, used especially for beer, approximately equal to 30 gal. Also used as a measure of weight for nails, equal to 100 lb.

kelvin (K) A scale of temperature measurement in which each degree is equal to $\frac{1}{273.16}$ of the interval between 0 K (absolute zero) and the triple point of water. K = °C+273.16. Named after William Thomson, Lord Kelvin (1824–1907).

kilo- Prefix meaning 1000; e.g., a kilogram (kg) is a unit of volume measurement equal to 1000 g.

kilocalorie (kcal or Cal) A unit of energy measurement representing the amount of heat required to raise 1 kg of water by 1 °C. Also called 'international calorie'. 1 kcal = 1000 cal. *See also* Calorie.

kilogram *see* Kilo-

kilometre (km) A unit of length equal to 1000 m.

kiloparsec A unit of distance used to measure distance between galactic bodies. 1 kiloparsec = 3260 light years (ly).

kilowatt (kW) A unit of power equal to 1000 watts (W).

kilowatt-hour (kWh) A unit of energy equal to the energy expended when a power of 1 kW is used for 1 hr.

knot (kn) A nautical unit of speed measurement equal to the velocity at which 1 nautical mile is travelled in 1 hr. 1 kn = 6076 ft per hour.

lakh An Indian counting unit equal to 100 000.

lambda (λ) A unit of volume measurement. 1 λ = 1 microlitre (10^{-6} litre).

league A unit of length equal to 3 mi.

light year (ly) A unit of length (distance) representing the distance travelled by electromagnetic waves (light) through space in 1 year. 1 light year = 9.4605×10^{12} km (or, in the UK, 6 billion miles; in the US, 6 trillion miles).

line A unit of length equal to $\frac{1}{12}$ in; 4 line = 1 barley-corn. It can also be used to measure button diameters, when 1 line = $\frac{1}{40}$ in.

litre (l) A unit of volume measurement equal to the volume of 1 kg of water at its maximum density. 1 litre = 1000 cm^3.

magnum A measure of volume, used especially for wine or champagne. In the UK, 1 magnum = $\frac{2}{5}$ UK gal; in the US, 1 magnum = $\frac{2}{5}$ US gal.

mega- Prefix meaning 1 million; e.g., a megaton is a unit of weight equal to 1 million tons.

megahertz (MHz) A unit of frequency (for radio) equal to 1 million cycles per second.

metre (m) A unit of length equal to 100 cm.

metres per minute (m/min) A unit of velocity measurement representing the number of metres travelled in 1 min.

metric system A system of measurement based on the metre.

micro- Prefix meaning 1 millionth; e.g., a microlitre is a unit of volume equal to 1 millionth of a litre.

micron (μm) A unit of length equal to $\frac{1}{1000}$ (0.001) mm. Also called the micrometre.

mile (mi) A unit of length equal to 1760 yd. Also called the statute mile in the UK.

nautical mile (n mi) A unit of length used in navigation. In the UK, 1 n mi = 6080 ft; in the metric system, 1 n mi (international) = 1852 m.

Also called the geographical mile.

sea mile A unit of length distinguished from the nautical mile. 1 sea mile = 1000 fathoms (6000 ft).

miles per hour (mph) A unit of velocity representing the number of miles travelled in 1 hr.

millennium A period of time equal to 1000 years.

milli- Prefix meaning 1 thousandth or $1/1000$; e.g., 1 millimetre (mm) is a unit of length equal to $1/1000$ (0.001) m.

minim A unit of volume, usually for liquids. In the UK, 1 minim = $1/480$ UK fl oz; in the US, 1 minim = $1/480$ US fl oz. The two should not be confused: 1 UK minim = 0.961 US minim.

minute

    geometric (') A unit of measure for plane angles. $1' = 1/60°$.

    time (m or min) A unit of time measurement equal to 60 s. 60 min = 1 hr.

month

    lunar A unit of time equal to 4 weeks (2 419 200 s).

    sidereal *see* Year, sidereal.

    tropical *see* Year, tropical.

nano- In the UK, a prefix meaning 1 thousand millionth (10^{-9}); in the US, meaning 1 billionth (10^{-9}). For example, in the UK, 1 nanometre = 1 thousand millionth of a metre; in the US, 1 nanometre = 1 billionth of a metre.

nautical mile *see* Mile.

newton (N) A unit of force equal to that creating an acceleration of 1 m per second when applied to a mass of 1 kg. This unit has replaced the dyne: $1 N = 10^5$ dynes. Named after Isaac Newton (1642–1727).

ohm (Ω) A unit of electrical resistance. One ohm equals the resistance across which a potential difference of 1 volt produces a current flow of 1 ampere. Named after G.S. Ohm (1787–1854).

ounce (oz) A unit of mass equal to ¹⁄₁₆ lb.

> **fluid ounce** A unit of liquid volume measurement. In the UK, 1 fl oz = ¹⁄₂₀ UK pt; in the US, 1 fl oz = ¹⁄₁₆ US pt.

> **metric ounce** A unit of mass equal to 25 g. Also called a Mounce.

> **ounce troy** A unit of mass in the troy system. Equal to ¹⁄₁₂ pound troy.

pace A unit of length/distance equal to 5 ft, used in ancient Rome.

palm A unit of length used in ancient Egypt, equal to the width of an average palm of the hand (4 digits).

parsec (pc) A unit of length used for measuring astronomical distances. 1 parsec = 3.26 light years (ly).

pascal (pa) A unit of pressure equal to the force of 1 N acting over an area of 1 m^2.

peck (pk) A unit of dry volume. In the UK, 1 peck = 2 UK gal; in the US, 1 peck = 2 US gal. The two should not be confused: 1 UK peck ≈ 1.032 US peck.

pennyweight (dwt) A unit of weight in the troy system equal to ¹⁄₂₀ ounce troy (25 grains).

perch A unit of length equal to 5½ yd. Also called a pole or a rod.

pi (π) Symbol and name representing the ratio of a circle's circumference to its diameter. Its value is approximately 3.14.

pica A unit of length, used by printers, approximately equal to ⅙ in.

pico- In the UK, a prefix meaning 1 billionth (10^{-12}); in the US, meaning 1 trillionth (10^{-12}). For example, in the UK, 1 picometre = 1 billionth of a metre; in the US, 1 picometre = 1 trillionth of a metre.

pint (pt) A unit of volume. In the UK, a pint measures either dry or liquid volume: 1 pt = ⅛ UK gal. In the US, two kinds of pint are used: 1 fl pt = ⅛ US gal; 1 dry pt = ¹⁄₆₄ US bu. These two should not be confused: 1 UK pt ≈ 1.2 US fl pt ≈ 1.03 US dry pt.

point A unit of length, used especially by printers, approximately equal to $\frac{1}{72}$ in.

pole Unit of length equal to 5½ yd. *See also* Perch; Rod.

pound (lb) A unit of mass equal to 453.59 g.

> **force pound** A unit of force equal to 32.174 poundals. Also called pound-force.
>
> **pound troy (lb tr)** A unit of mass in the troy system. 1 pound troy = 12 ounces troy.

poundal A unit of force equal to that needed to give an acceleration of 1 ft per second to a mass of 1 lb.

PSI Pounds per square inch: a unit for measuring pressure. 1 PSI equals the pressure resulting from a force of 1 force pound acting over an area of 1 in². *See also* Pound.

quart (qt) A unit of volume, usually for liquids. In the UK, 1 qt = 2 UK pt; in the US, 1 qt = 2 US fl pt. The two should not be confused: 1 UK qt ≈ 1.2 US qt.

> **dry quart (dry qt)** A unit of measure for dry (solid) volume in US.

reputed quart A unit of volume, used especially for wine, equalling ⅙ of a Winchester wine gallon.
Winchester quart A unit of fluid volume equal to 2.5 litres.

quarter (qr)

mass quarter A unit of mass. In the UK, 1 quarter = ¼ UK hundredweight (28 lb); in the US, 1 quarter = ¼ US ton (500 lb).

quarter troy (qr tr) A unit of weight equal to 25 troy pounds.

volume quarter A unit of volume, in the UK, equal to 8 UK bu.

quintal (q) A unit of mass equal to 100 kg or 100 lb. Called the short hundredweight in the US.

rad A short form of radian, a unit of measure for plane angles. *See also* Centrad.

ream A unit of volume, used to measure paper in bulk. 1 ream equals about 500 sheets.

rod

area rod A unit of area equal to 30¼ yd². Also called a square perch or a square pole.

length rod A unit of length equal to 5½ yd. *See also* Perch; Pole.

rood A unit of area equal to ¼ acre (1210 yd²).

score A counting unit equal to 20 times the original unit.

scruple A unit of mass in apothecaries' system equal to 20 grains.

second A unit of time equal to ⅟₆₀ minute.

geometric (′) A measure of plane angle equal to

⅟₃₆₀° and ⅟₆₀″.

orbital A unit of time equal to ⅟₃₁ ₅₅₇ of the tropical year 1900. Also called Ephemeris second.

sidereal A unit of time equal to ⅟₈₆ ₄₀₀ of the interval needed for one complete rotation of the Earth on its axis.

square units (sq or ²) These are arrived at by multiplying a number by itself. To find the area of, e.g. a square or rectangle, length and breadth are multiplied together to give the area, which is measured in square units.

stere A unit of volume, especially used for measuring timber. 1 stere = 1 m³.

stone (st) A unit of mass used in the UK. 1 st = 14 lb.

tablespoon (tbsp) A unit of volume used in cooking and equal to 1.5 centilitres (3 tsp). 16 tbsp = 1 cup.

teaspoon (tsp) A unit of volume used in cooking and equal to 0.5 centilitre. 3 tsp = 1 tbsp.

tera- In the UK, a prefix meaning 1 billion (10^{12}); in the US, meaning 1 trillion (10^{12}). For example, in the UK, 1 terametre = 1 billion metres; in the US, 1 terametre = 1 trillion metres.

ton A unit of mass. In the UK, 1 ton = 2240 lb. Called a long ton in the US. In the US, 1 ton = 2000 lb. Called a short ton in the UK.

ton troy (ton tr) A unit of mass equal to 2000 pounds troy.

tonne (t) A unit of mass equal to 1000 kg. Also called a metric ton.

tonne of coal equivalent A measure of energy

production/consumption based on the premise that
1 tonne of coal provides 8000 kilowatt-hours (kWh)
of energy.

trillion In UK, equal to 10^{18}; in US, equal to 10^{12}.

troy system A system of mass measurement based
on the 20-oz pound and the 20-pennyweight ounce.

volt (V) A unit of electromotive force and potential
difference. Equal to the difference in potential between
two points of a conducting wire carrying a constant
current of 1 ampere (A), when the power released
between the points is 1 watt (W). Named after
Alessandro Volta (1745–1827).

watt (W) A unit of power equal to that available
when 1 J of energy is expended in 1 s.
1 W = 1 volt-ampere; 746 W = 1 horsepower (hp).
Named after James Watt (1736–1819).

X-unit (x or XU) A unit of length used especially for
measuring wavelength. 1 x-unit $\approx 10^{-3}$ ångström
(10^{-13} m).

yard (yd) A unit of length equal to 3 ft (36 in).

yards per minute (ypm) A unit of velocity
representing the number of yards travelled in 1 min.

year A unit of time measurement determined by the
revolution of the Earth around the Sun.

    anomalistic year Equals the time interval between
two consecutive passages of the Earth through its
perihelion (365 days, 6 hr, 13 min, 53 s).

    sidereal year Equals the time in which it takes the

Earth to revolve around the Sun from one fixed point (usually a star) back to the same point (365 days, 6 hr, 9 min, 9 s).

tropical year Equals the time interval between two consecutive passages of the Sun, in one direction, through the Earth's equatorial plane (or from vernal equinox to vernal equinox; 365 days, 5 hr, 48 min, 46 s).

Unit systems

International System of Units
The International System of Units (or Système International d'Unités – SI) is the current form of the metric system that has been in use since 1960. In the UK, the SI system is used in education, science and, increasingly, in everyday life.

Base units
There are seven base units in SI:

Unit	Symbol	Quantity
metre	m	length/distance
kilogram	kg	mass
ampere	A	electric current
kelvin	K	temperature
candela	cd	luminosity
second	s/sec	time
mole	mol	amount of substance

Supplementary units
There are also two supplementary units:

Unit	Symbol	Quantity
radian	rad	plane angle
steradian	sr	solid angle

Derived units
In addition, the system uses derived units, which are expressed in terms of the seven base units above. For example, velocity is given in metres per second (m/s, ms^{-1}). Other derived units in SI are referred to by special names. For example, the watt (W) is a unit of power; the joule (J) is a unit of energy.

Imperial system of units

Length 1 inch (in or ")				
1 foot (ft or ')	12 in			
1 yard (yd)	36 in	3 ft		
1 fathom (fm)	72 in	6 ft	2 yd	
1 chain (ch)		66 ft	22 yd	
1 furlong			220 yd	
1 mile (mi)		5 280 ft	1760 yd	
Area 1 square inch (in²)				
1 square foot (ft²)	144 in²			
1 square yard (yd²)		9 ft²		
1 square chain (ch²)			484 yd²	
1 acre			4840 yd²	
1 square mile (mi²)	640 acres			
Volume 1 cubic in (in³)				
1 fluid ounce (fl oz)				
1 pint (pt)	20 fl oz			
1 quart (qt)	40 fl oz	2 pt		
1 gallon (gal)		8 pt	4 qt	
1 cubic foot (ft³)	1728 in³			
1 cubic yard (yd³)	46 656 in³	27ft³		
Weight 1 grain (gr)				
1 ounce (oz)	437.5 gr			
1 pound (lb)		16 oz		
1 stone (st)			14 lb	
1 ton		35 840 oz	2240 lb	

1: Numbers

Named numbers

Many numbers have names. Some of these names are in everyday use, others apply in more specialised areas such as music and multiple births; and for sums of money. Some names for specialised numbers have the same first part (prefix). These prefixes indicate the number to which the name refers.

Everyday use

1/10	Tithe
2	Pair, couple, brace
6	Half a dozen
12	Dozen
13	Baker's dozen
20	Score
50	Half century
100	Century
144	Gross

Musicians

1	Soloist
2	Duet
3	Trio
4	Quartet
5	Quintet
6	Sextet
7	Septet
8	Octet

Multiple births

2	Twins
3	Triplets
4	Quadruplets (quads)
5	Quintuplets (quins)
6	Sextuplets

Slang for money

£25	Pony
£100	Century
£500	Monkey
£1000	Grand

Numerical prefixes

Prefixes in numerical order

$1/10$	Deci-	**7**	Hept-, hepta-, sept-, septi-, septem-
$1/2$	Semi-, hemi-, demi-	**8**	Oct-, octa-, octo-
1	Uni-	**9**	Non-, nona-, ennea-
2	Bi-, di-	**10**	Dec-, deca-
3	Tri-, ter-	**11**	Hendeca-, undec-, undeca-
4	Tetra-, tetr-, tessera-, quadri-, quadr-	**12**	Dodeca-
5	Pent-, penta-, quinqu-, quinque-, quint-	**15**	Quindeca-
6	Sex-, sexi-, hex-, hexa-	**20**	Icos-, icosa-, icosi-

Prefixes in alphabetical order

Bi-,	**2**	Pent-, penta-	**5**
Dec-, deca-	**10**	Quadr-, quadri-	**4**
Deci-	$1/10$	Quindeca-	**15**
Demi-	$1/2$	Quinqu-, quinque-	**5**
Di-	**2**	Quint-	**5**
Dodeca-	**12**	Semi-	$1/2$
Ennea-	**9**	Sept-, septem-, septi-	**7**
Hemi-	$1/2$	Sex-, sexi-	**6**
Hendeca-	**11**	Ter-	**3**
Hept-, Hepta-	**7**	Tessera-	**4**
Hex-, hexa-	**6**	Tetr-, tetra-	**4**
Icos-, icosa-, icosi-	**20**	Tri-	**3**
Non-, nona-	**9**	Undec-, undeca-	**11**
Oct-, octa-, octo-	**8**	Uni-	**1**

Prefixes and their values

Prefixes in order of value	Value
*Atto-	0.000 000 000 000 000 001
*Femto-	0.000 000 000 000 001
*Pico-	0.000 000 000 001
*Nano-	0.000 000 001
*Micro-	0.000 001
*Milli-	0.001
*Centi-	0.01
*Deci-	0.1
Semi-, hemi-, demi-	0.5
Uni-	1
Bi-, di-	2
Tri-, ter-	3
Tetra-, tetr-, tessera-, quadri-, quadr-	4
Pent-, penta-, quinqu-, quinque-, quint-	5
Sex-, sexi-, hex-, hexa-	6

* approved for use with the SI system

Prefixes in numerical order	Value
Hept-, hepta-, sept-, septi-, septem-	7
Oct-, octa-, octo-	8
Non-, nona-, ennea-	9
Dec-, deca-	10
Hendeca-, undec-, undeca-	11
Dodeca-	12
Quindeca-	15
Icos-, icosa-, icosi-	20
Hect-, hecto-	100
*Kilo-	1 000
Myria-	10 000
*Mega-	1 000 000
*Giga-	1 000 000 000
*Tera-	1 000 000 000 000

Historic number systems

Different civilisations have developed their own systems for writing numbers. Here we show numerals from eight such systems.

	Roman	Arabic	Chinese	Hindu
1	I	١	一	?
2	II	٢	二	?
3	III	٣	三	?
4	IV	٤	四	?
5	V	٥	五	?
6	VI	٦	六	?
7	VII	٧	七	?
8	VIII	٨	八	?
9	IX	٩	九	?
10	X	١٠	十	?٠
50	L	٥٠	五十	?٠
100	C	١٠٠	百	?٠٠
500	D	٥٠٠	百五	?٠٠
1000	M	١٠٠٠	千	?٠٠٠

Babylonian	**Egyptian**	**Hebrew**	**Japanese**
𒁹	𓏺	א	一
𒈫	𓏻	ב	二
𒐈	𓏼	ג	三
𒐉	𓏽	ד	四
𒐊	𓏾	ה	五
𒐋	𓏿	ו	六
𒑂	𓐀	ז	七
𒑄	𓐁	ח	八
𒑆	𓐂	ט	九
𒌋	𓎆	י	十
𒐐	𓎆𓎆𓎆𓎆𓎆	כ	五十
𒁹𒐏	𓍢	ק	百
𒐊𒈨	𓍢𓍢𓍢𓍢𓍢	ר	五百
𒁹𒇷	𓆼	'א	千

Roman number system

The Roman numeral system is a method of notation in which the capitals are modelled on ancient Roman inscriptions. The numerals are represented by seven capital letters of the alphabet:

I	one
V	five
X	ten
L	fifty
C	one hundred
D	five hundred
M	one thousand

These letters are the foundation of the system; they are combined in order to form all numbers. If a letter is preceded by another of lesser value (e.g., IX), the value of the combined form is the difference between the values of each letter (e.g., IX = X (10) − I (1) = 9).

To determine the value of a string of Roman numbers (letters), find the pairs in the string (those beginning with a lower value) and determine their values, then add these to the values of the other letters in the string:

MCMXCI = M+CM+XC+I = 1000+900+90+1 = 1991

A dash over a letter multiplies the value by 1000 (e.g. $\overline{V}$ = 5000).

1 I	12 XII	35 XXXV	100 C
2 II	13 XIII	40 XL	200 CC
3 III	14 XIV	45 XLV	300 CCC
4 IV or IIII	15 XV	50 L	400 CD
5 V	16 XVI	55 LV	500 D
6 VI	17 XVII	60 LX	600 DC
7 VII	18 XVIII	65 LXV	700 DCC
8 VIII	19 XIX	70 LXX	800 DCCC
9 IX	20 XX	75 LXXV	900 CM
10 X	25 XXV	80 LXXX	1000 M
11 XI	30 XXX	90 XC	2000 MM

Mathematical symbols

$+$	plus or positive	$\geqslant$	greater than or equal to
$-$	minus or negative	$\leqslant$	less than or equal to
$\pm$	plus or minus, positive or negative	$\gg$	much greater than
$\times$	multiplied by	$\ll$	much less than
$\div$	divided by	$\sqrt{}$	square root
$=$	equal to	∞	infinity
$\equiv$	identically equal to	$\propto$	proportional to
$\neq$	not equal to	$\sum$	sum of
$\not\equiv$	not identically equal to	$\prod$	product of
$\approx$	approximately equal to	Δ	difference
$\sim$	of the order of or similar to	$\therefore$	therefore
$>$	greater than	$\angle$	angle
$<$	less than	$\parallel$	parallel to
$\not>$	not greater than	$\perp$	perpendicular to
$\not<$	not less than	$:$	is to

Arithmetic operations

The four basic arithmetic operations are addition, subtraction, multiplication and division. Each part of an arithmetic operation has a specific name.

Addition

29 Addend

+6 Addend

35 Sum

Subtraction

74 Minuend

-16 Subtrahend

58 Difference

Multiplication

46 Multiplicand

x9 Multiplier

414 Product

Division

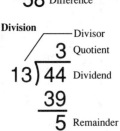

Divisor

3 Quotient

13)44 Dividend

39

5 Remainder

Fraction

$\frac{5}{8}$ $\frac{5}{8}$ Numerator / Denominator

Simple (or vulgar) fraction

$\frac{9}{7}$ $\frac{9}{7}$ Numerator / Denominator

Binary numbers

The binary system is formulated on a base of 2, or on a sum of powers of 2. For example, the number 101011 is equal to $2^5 + 0 + 2^3 + 0 + 2^1 + 2^0$; in the decimal system, this number equals 43. The system is used frequently in computer applications.

In describing computer storage, 1 bit = 1 binary digit; 1 byte = 8 bits in most systems; 1 megabyte (MB) = 1 048 576 bytes. The table below shows other decimal/binary equivalents.

Decimal	Binary	Decimal	Binary
1	1	21	10101
2	10	30	11110
3	11	40	101000
4	100	50	110010
5	101	60	111100
6	110	90	1011010
7	111	100	1100100
8	1000	200	11001000
9	1001	300	100101100
10	1010	400	110010000
11	1011	500	111110100
12	1100	600	1001011000
13	1101	900	1110000100
14	1110	1 000	1111101000
15	1111	2 000	11111010000
16	10000	4 000	111110100000
17	10001	5 000	1001110001000
18	10010	10 000	10011100010000
19	10011	20 000	100111000100000
20	10100	100 000	11000011010100000

Computer coding systems

ASCII (American Standard Code for Information Interchange) is an international coding system of character representation. Its 256 codes represent computer commands and letters of the alphabet. Hexadecimal is a system of numbering based on 16 digits (as opposed to 10 in the decimal system): 1 to 9 and A to F.

Binary, ASCII and hexadecimal systems are used in computer programming.

The table below shows character equivalents in decimal, hexadecimal and ASCII systems.

Dec	Hex	ASCII	Dec	Hex	ASCII
000	00	NUL	016	10	DLE
001	01	SOH	017	11	DC1
002	02	STX	018	12	DC2
003	03	ETX	019	13	DC3
004	04	EOT	020	14	DC4
005	05	ENQ	021	15	NAK
006	06	ACK	022	16	SYN
007	07	BEL	023	17	ETB
008	08	BS	024	18	CAN
009	09	HT	025	19	EM
010	0A	LF	026	1A	SUB
011	0B	VT	027	1B	ESCAPE
012	0C	FF	028	1C	FS
013	0D	CR	029	1D	GS
014	0E	SO	030	1E	RS
015	0F	SI	031	1F	US

Dec	Hex	ASCII	Dec	Hex	ASCII
032	20	SPACE	057	39	9
033	21	!	058	3A	:
034	22	"	059	3B	;
035	23	#	060	3C	<
036	24	$	061	3D	=
037	25	%	062	3E	>
038	26	&	063	3F	?
039	27	'	064	40	@
040	28	(	065	41	A
041	29	)	066	42	B
042	2A	*	067	43	C
043	2B	+	068	44	D
044	2C	,	069	45	E
045	2D	−	070	46	F
046	2E	.	071	47	G
047	2F	/	072	48	H
048	30	0	073	49	I
049	31	1	074	4A	J
050	32	2	075	4B	K
051	33	3	076	4C	L
052	34	4	077	4D	M
053	35	5	078	4E	N
054	36	6	079	4F	O
055	37	7	080	50	P
056	38	8	081	51	Q

Dec	Hex	ASCII	Dec	Hex	ASCII
082	52	R	107	6B	k
083	53	S	108	6C	l
084	54	T	109	6D	m
085	55	U	110	6E	n
086	56	V	111	6F	o
087	57	W	112	70	p
088	58	X	113	71	q
089	59	Y	114	72	r
090	5A	Z	115	73	s
091	5B	[	116	74	t
092	5C	\	117	75	u
093	5D	]	118	76	v
094	5E	^	119	77	w
095	5F	_	120	78	x
096	60	`	121	79	y
097	61	a	122	7A	z
098	62	b	123	7B	{
099	63	c	124	7C	|
100	64	d	125	7D	}
101	65	e	126	7E	~
102	66	f	127	7F	DEL
103	67	g			
104	68	h			
105	69	i			
106	6A	j			

Fractions, decimals and percentages

Fraction					Decimal	Percentage
$^1/_9$					0.111 111	111.11%
$^1/_7$					0.142 857	14.29%
$^1/_6$					0.166 667	16.67%
$^1/_5$					0.2	20.00%
$^2/_9$					0.222 222	22.22%
$^2/_7$					0.285 714	28.58%
$^3/_9$	$^2/_6$	$^1/_3$			0.333 333	33.33%
$^2/_5$					0.4	40.00%
$^3/_7$					0.428 571	42.86%
$^4/_9$					0.444 444	44.44%
$^3/_6$					0.5	50.00%
$^5/_9$					0.555 555	55.56%
$^4/_7$					0.571 429	57.14%
$^3/_5$					0.6	60.00%
$^6/_9$	$^4/_6$	$^2/_3$			0.666 666	66.67%
$^5/_7$					0.714 286	71.43%
$^7/_9$					0.777 778	77.78%
$^4/_5$					0.8	80.00%
$^5/_6$					0.833 333	83.33%
$^6/_7$					0.857 143	85.71%
$^8/_9$					0.888 889	88.89%
$^9/_9$	$^7/_7$	$^6/_6$	$^5/_5$	$^3/_3$	0.1	100%

Fraction	Decimal	Percentage
$1/64$	0.015 625	1.56%
$2/64$ $1/32$	0.031 25	3.13%
$3/64$	0.046875	4.69%
$4/64$ $2/32$ $1/16$	0.062 5	6.25%
$5/64$	0.078 125	7.81%
$6/64$ $3/32$	0.093 75	9.38%
$7/64$	0.109 375	10.94%
$8/64$ $4/32$ $2/16$ $1/8$	0.125	12.50%
$9/64$	0.140 625	14.06%
$10/64$ $5/32$	0.156 25	15.63%
$11/64$	0.171 875	17.19%
$12/64$ $6/32$ $3/16$	0.187 5	18.75%
$13/64$	0.203 125	20.31%
$14/64$ $7/32$	0.218 75	21.88%
$15/64$	0.234 375	23.44%
$16/64$ $8/32$ $4/16$ $2/8$ $1/4$	0.25	25.00%
$17/64$	0.265 625	26.56%
$18/64$ $9/32$	0.281 25	28.13%
$19/64$	0.296 875	29.69%
$20/64$ $10/32$ $5/16$	0.312 5	31.25%
$21/64$	0.328 125	32.81%
$22/64$ $11/32$	0.343 75	34.38%

Fractions, decimals and percentages (continued)

Fraction							Decimal	Percentage
$^{23}/_{64}$							0.359 375	35.94%
$^{24}/_{64}$	$^{12}/_{32}$	$^{6}/_{16}$	$^{3}/_{8}$				0.375	37.50%
$^{25}/_{64}$							0.390 625	39.06%
$^{26}/_{64}$	$^{12}/_{32}$						0.406 25	40.63%
$^{27}/_{64}$							0.421 875	42.19%
$^{28}/_{64}$	$^{14}/_{32}$	$^{7}/_{16}$					0.437 5	43.75%
$^{29}/_{64}$							0.453 125	45.31%
$^{30}/_{64}$	$^{15}/_{32}$						0.468 75	46.88%
$^{31}/_{64}$							0.484 375	48.44%
$^{32}/_{64}$	$^{16}/_{32}$	$^{8}/_{16}$	$^{4}/_{8}$	$^{2}/_{4}$	$^{1}/_{2}$		0.5	50.00%
$^{33}/_{64}$							0.515 625	51.56%
$^{34}/_{64}$	$^{17}/_{32}$						0.531 25	53.13%
$^{35}/_{64}$							0.546 875	54.69%
$^{36}/_{64}$	$^{18}/_{32}$	$^{9}/_{16}$					0.562 5	56.25%
$^{37}/_{64}$							0.578 125	57.81%
$^{38}/_{64}$	$^{19}/_{32}$						0.593 75	59.37%
$^{39}/_{64}$							0.609 375	60.94%
$^{40}/_{64}$	$^{20}/_{32}$	$^{10}/_{16}$	$^{5}/_{8}$				0.625	62.50%
$^{41}/_{64}$							0.640 625	64.06%
$^{42}/_{64}$	$^{21}/_{32}$						0.656 25	65.63%
$^{43}/_{64}$							0.671 875	67.19%
$^{44}/_{64}$	$^{22}/_{32}$	$^{11}/_{16}$					0.687 5	68.75%

Fraction						Decimal	Percentage
$^{45}/_{64}$						0.703 125	70.31%
$^{46}/_{64}$	$^{23}/_{32}$					0.718 75	71.38%
$^{47}/_{64}$						0.734 375	73.44%
$^{48}/_{64}$	$^{24}/_{32}$	$^{12}/_{16}$	$^{6}/_{8}$	$^{3}/_{4}$		0.75	75.00%
$^{49}/_{64}$						0.765 625	76.56%
$^{50}/_{64}$	$^{25}/_{32}$					0.781 25	78.13%
$^{51}/_{64}$						0.796 875	79.69%
$^{52}/_{64}$	$^{26}/_{32}$	$^{13}/_{16}$				0.812 5	81.25%
$^{53}/_{64}$						0.828 125	82.81%
$^{54}/_{64}$	$^{27}/_{32}$					0.843 75	84.38%
$^{55}/_{64}$						0.859 375	85.94%
$^{56}/_{64}$	$^{28}/_{32}$	$^{14}/_{16}$	$^{7}/_{8}$			0.875	87.50%
$^{57}/_{64}$						0.890 625	89.06%
$^{58}/_{64}$	$^{29}/_{32}$					0.906 25	90.63%
$^{59}/_{64}$						0.921 875	92.19%
$^{60}/_{64}$	$^{30}/_{32}$	$^{15}/_{16}$				0.937 5	93.75%
$^{61}/_{64}$						0.953 125	95.31%
$^{62}/_{64}$	$^{31}/_{32}$					0.968 75	96.88%
$^{63}/_{64}$						0.984 375	98.44%
$^{64}/_{64}$	$^{32}/_{32}$	$^{16}/_{16}$	$^{8}/_{8}$	$^{4}/_{4}$	$^{2}/_{2}$	1	100%

Prime numbers

These are whole numbers that have only two factors – the number itself and the number 1. The only even prime number is 2: all other prime numbers are odd.

There are an infinite number of prime numbers. The first 126 are given below. The number at the foot of the table is the largest prime known in 1952. The largest prime known in 1983 has 39 751 digits.

2	47	109	191	269	353	439	523	617
3	53	113	193	271	359	443	541	619
5	59	127	197	277	367	449	547	631
7	61	131	199	281	373	457	557	641
11	67	137	211	283	379	461	563	643
13	71	139	223	293	383	463	569	647
17	73	149	227	307	389	467	571	653
19	79	151	229	311	397	479	577	659
23	83	157	233	313	401	487	587	661
29	89	163	239	317	409	491	593	673
31	97	167	241	331	419	499	599	677
37	101	173	251	337	421	503	601	683
41	103	179	257	347	431	509	607	691
43	107	181	263	349	433	521	613	701

1701411834604692317316873037158841 05727

Fibonacci sequence

Each number in a Fibonacci is the sum of the two numbers preceding it. The sequence can therefore be built up using simple addition. Below is an example of a Fibonacci sequence.

$0+1 = \mathbf{1}$	$987+610 = \mathbf{1597}$
$1+1 = \mathbf{2}$	$1597+987 = \mathbf{2584}$
$2+1 = \mathbf{3}$	$2584+1597 = \mathbf{4181}$
$3+2 = \mathbf{5}$	$4181+2584 = \mathbf{6765}$
$5+3 = \mathbf{8}$	$6765+4181 = \mathbf{10\ 946}$
$8+5 = \mathbf{13}$	$10\ 946+6765 = \mathbf{17\ 711}$
$13+8 = \mathbf{21}$	$17\ 711+10\ 946 = \mathbf{28\ 657}$
$21+13 = \mathbf{34}$	$28\ 657+17\ 711 = \mathbf{46\ 368}$
$34+21 = \mathbf{55}$	$46\ 368+28\ 657 = \mathbf{75\ 025}$
$55+34 = \mathbf{89}$	$75\ 025+46\ 368 = \mathbf{121\ 393}$
$89+55 = \mathbf{144}$	$121\ 393+75\ 025 = \mathbf{196\ 418}$
$144+89 = \mathbf{233}$	$196\ 418+121\ 393 = \mathbf{317\ 811}$
$233+144 = \mathbf{377}$	$317\ 811+196\ 418 = \mathbf{514\ 229}$
$377+233 = \mathbf{610}$	$514\ 229+317\ 811 = \mathbf{832\ 040}$
$610+377 = \mathbf{987}$	$832\ 040+514\ 299 = \mathbf{1\ 346\ 339}$

Square and cube roots

*Accurate to 3 decimal places – they have not been rounded up or down.

Square and cube* roots of 1 to 25		
	√	³√
1	1.000	1.000
2	1.414	1.259
3	1.732	1.442
4	2.000	1.587
5	2.236	1.709
6	2.449	1.817
7	2.645	1.912
8	2.828	2.000
9	3.000	2.080
10	3.162	2.154
11	3.316	2.223
12	3.464	2.289
13	3.605	2.351
14	3.741	2.410
15	3.873	2.466
16	4.000	2.519
17	4.123	2.571
18	4.242	2.620
19	4.358	2.668
20	4.472	2.714
21	4.582	2.758
22	4.690	2.802
23	4.795	2.843
24	4.899	2.884
25	5.000	2.924

Square and cube* roots of 26 to 50		
	√	³√
26	5.099	2.962
27	5.196	3.000
28	5.291	3.036
29	5.385	3.072
30	5.477	3.107
31	5.567	3.141
32	5.656	3.174
33	5.744	3.207
34	5.831	3.239
35	5.916	3.271
36	6.000	3.301
37	6.082	3.332
38	6.614	3.361
39	6.245	3.391
40	6.324	3.419
41	6.403	3.448
42	6.480	3.476
43	6.557	3.503
44	6.633	3.530
45	6.708	3.556
46	6.782	3.583
47	6.855	3.608
48	6.928	3.634
49	7.000	3.659
50	7.071	3.684

Square and cube* roots of 51 to 75				Square and cube* roots of 76 to 100		
	$\sqrt{}$	$\sqrt[3]{}$			$\sqrt{}$	$\sqrt[3]{}$
51	7.141	3.708		76	8.717	4.235
52	7.211	3.732		77	8.775	4.254
53	7.280	3.756		78	8.831	4.272
54	7.348	3.779		79	8.888	4.290
55	7.416	3.802		80	8.944	4.308
56	7.483	3.825		81	9.000	4.326
57	7.549	3.848		82	9.055	4.344
58	7.615	3.870		83	9.110	4.362
59	7.681	3.893		84	9.165	4.379
60	7.746	3.913		85	9.219	4.396
61	7.810	3.936		86	9.273	4.414
62	7.874	3.957		87	9.327	4.431
63	7.937	3.979		88	9.380	4.447
64	8.000	4.000		89	9.434	4.464
65	8.062	4.020		90	9.486	4.481
66	8.124	4.041		91	9.539	4.497
67	8.185	4.061		92	9.591	4.514
68	8.246	4.081		93	9.643	4.530
69	8.306	4.101		94	9.695	4.546
70	8.366	4.121		95	9.746	4.562
71	8.426	4.140		96	9.798	4.578
72	8.485	4.160		97	9.848	4.594
73	8.544	4.179		98	9.899	4.610
74	8.602	4.198		99	9.949	4.626
75	8.660	4.217		100	10.000	4.641

Multiplication tables

×2		×3		×4		×5		×6	
1	2	1	3	1	4	1	5	1	6
2	4	2	6	2	8	2	10	2	12
3	6	3	9	3	12	3	15	3	18
4	8	4	12	4	16	4	20	4	24
5	10	5	15	5	20	5	25	5	30
6	12	6	18	6	24	6	30	6	36
7	14	7	21	7	28	7	35	7	42
8	16	8	24	8	32	8	40	8	48
9	18	9	27	9	36	9	45	9	54
10	20	10	30	10	40	10	50	10	60
11	22	11	33	11	44	11	55	11	66
12	24	12	36	12	48	12	60	12	72
13	26	13	39	13	52	13	65	13	78
14	28	14	42	14	56	14	70	14	84
15	30	15	45	15	60	15	75	15	90
16	32	16	48	16	64	16	80	16	96
17	34	17	51	17	68	17	85	17	102
18	36	18	54	18	72	18	90	18	108
19	38	19	57	19	76	19	95	19	114
25	50	25	75	25	100	25	125	20	150
35	70	35	105	35	140	35	175	35	210
45	90	45	135	45	180	45	225	45	270
55	110	55	165	55	220	55	275	55	330
65	130	65	195	65	260	65	325	65	390
75	150	75	225	75	300	75	375	75	450
85	170	85	255	85	340	85	425	85	510
95	190	95	285	95	380	95	475	95	570

×7		×8		×9		×10		×11	
1	7	1	8	1	9	1	10	1	11
2	14	2	16	2	18	2	20	2	22
3	21	3	24	3	27	3	30	3	33
4	28	4	32	4	36	4	40	4	44
5	35	5	40	5	45	5	50	5	55
6	42	6	48	6	54	6	60	6	66
7	49	7	56	7	63	7	70	7	77
8	56	8	64	8	72	8	80	8	88
9	63	9	72	9	81	9	90	9	99
10	70	10	80	10	90	10	100	10	110
11	77	11	88	11	99	11	110	11	121
12	84	12	96	12	108	12	120	12	132
13	91	13	104	13	117	13	130	13	143
14	98	14	112	14	126	14	140	14	154
15	105	15	120	15	135	15	150	15	165
16	112	16	128	16	144	16	160	16	176
17	119	17	136	17	153	17	170	17	187
18	126	18	144	18	162	18	180	18	198
19	133	19	152	19	171	19	190	19	209
25	175	25	200	25	225	25	250	20	275
35	245	35	280	35	315	35	350	35	385
45	315	45	360	45	405	45	450	45	495
55	385	55	440	55	495	55	550	55	605
65	455	65	520	65	585	65	650	65	715
75	525	75	600	75	675	75	750	75	825
85	595	85	680	85	765	85	850	85	935
95	665	95	760	95	855	95	950	95	1045

Multiplication tables (continued)

×12		×13		×14		×15		×16	
1	12	1	13	1	14	1	15	1	16
2	24	2	26	2	28	2	30	2	32
3	36	3	39	3	42	3	45	3	48
4	48	4	52	4	56	4	60	4	64
5	60	5	65	5	70	5	75	5	80
6	72	6	78	6	84	6	90	6	96
7	84	7	91	7	98	7	105	7	112
8	96	8	104	8	112	8	120	8	128
9	108	9	117	9	126	9	135	9	144
10	120	10	130	10	140	10	150	10	160
11	132	11	143	11	154	11	165	11	176
12	144	12	156	12	168	12	180	12	192
13	156	13	169	13	182	13	195	13	208
14	168	14	182	14	196	14	210	14	224
15	180	15	195	15	210	15	225	15	240
16	192	16	208	16	224	16	240	16	256
17	204	17	221	17	238	17	255	17	272
18	216	18	234	18	252	18	270	18	288
19	228	19	247	19	266	19	285	19	304
25	300	25	325	25	350	25	375	20	400
35	420	35	455	35	490	35	525	35	560
45	540	45	585	45	630	45	675	45	720
55	660	55	715	55	770	55	825	55	880
65	780	65	845	65	910	65	975	65	1040
75	900	75	975	75	1050	75	1125	75	1200
85	1020	85	1105	85	1190	85	1275	85	1360
95	1140	95	1235	95	1330	95	1425	95	1520

×17		×18		×19		×20		×21	
1	17	1	18	1	19	1	20	1	21
2	34	2	36	2	38	2	40	2	42
3	51	3	54	3	57	3	60	3	63
4	68	4	72	4	76	4	80	4	84
5	85	5	90	5	95	5	100	5	105
6	102	6	108	6	114	6	120	6	126
7	119	7	126	7	133	7	140	7	147
8	136	8	144	8	152	8	160	8	168
9	153	9	162	9	171	9	180	9	189
10	170	10	180	10	190	10	200	10	210
11	187	11	198	11	209	11	220	11	231
12	204	12	216	12	228	12	240	12	252
13	221	13	234	13	247	13	260	13	273
14	238	14	252	14	266	14	280	14	294
15	255	15	270	15	285	15	300	15	315
16	272	16	288	16	304	16	320	16	336
17	289	17	306	17	323	17	340	17	357
18	306	18	324	18	342	18	360	18	378
19	323	19	342	19	361	19	380	19	399
25	425	25	450	25	475	25	500	20	525
35	595	35	630	35	665	35	700	35	735
45	765	45	810	45	855	45	900	45	945
55	935	55	990	55	1045	55	1100	55	1155
65	1105	65	1170	65	1235	65	1300	65	1365
75	1275	75	1350	75	1425	75	1500	75	1575
85	1445	85	1530	85	1615	85	1700	85	1785
95	1615	95	1710	95	1805	95	1900	95	1995

Multiplication grid

Below is a quick-reference grid giving products and quotients. It can be used for either multiplication or division.

Row	Column 1	2	3	4	5	6	7	8	9	10	11	12
1	1	2	3	4	5	6	7	8	9	10	11	12
2	2	4	6	8	10	12	14	16	18	20	22	24
3	3	6	9	12	15	18	21	24	27	30	33	36
4	4	8	12	16	20	24	28	32	36	40	44	48
5	5	10	15	20	25	30	35	40	45	50	55	60
6	6	12	18	24	30	36	42	48	54	60	66	72
7	7	14	21	28	35	42	49	56	63	70	77	84
8	8	16	24	32	40	48	56	64	72	80	88	96
9	9	18	27	36	45	54	63	72	81	90	99	108
10	10	20	30	40	50	60	70	80	90	100	110	120
11	11	22	33	44	55	66	77	88	99	110	121	132
12	12	24	36	48	60	72	84	96	108	120	132	144

Multiplication

To multiply 6 by 9, for example, scan down column six until you reach row nine. The number in the square where column six intersects row nine is the product, 54.

Division

To divide 56 by 8, scan down column eight to find 56 (the dividend) then scan across to find out the row number. This is the quotient, 7.

Interest

Interest refers to the charge made for borrowing money.
It is usually expressed in terms of percentage rates.
There are two types of interest: simple interest and
compound interest.

Simple interest

This type of interest is calculated on the amount of
money originally loaned (the principal). The formula
used to calculate simple interest is:

$$I = \frac{P \times R \times T}{100}$$

I is interest, P is principal, R is the percentage rate per
unit time, and T is the length of time (measured in
units) over which the money is invested or loaned.

The final sum – or amount of money to which the
principal will grow – is figured using the formula:

$$S \text{ (sum)} = P\left(1 + \frac{R \times T}{100}\right)$$

Compound interest

Unlike simple interest, which is paid only on the
principal, compound interest is paid also on the
previous interest earned. Thus the sum – or amount to
which the principal will grow – increases at a much
faster rate than with simple interest.

Compound interest is figured using the formula:

$$S = P(1 + i)^n$$

The 'i' represents the periodic interest; 'n' is the
number of periods.

Simple interest

Simple interest (in pounds) to add to £1000 (percent per annum)

	2.5%	3%	3.5%	4%
1 day	0.069	0.083	0.097	0.111
2 days	0.139	0.167	0.194	0.222
3 days	0.208	0.250	0.292	0.333
4 days	0.278	0.333	0.389	0.444
5 days	0.347	0.417	0.486	0.556
6 days	0.417	0.500	0.583	0.667
30 days	2.083	2.500	2.917	3.333
60 days	4.167	5.000	5.833	6.667
90 days	6.250	7.500	8.750	10.000
180 days	12.500	15.000	17.500	20.000
360 days	25.000	30.000	35.000	40.000

Simple interest (in pounds) added on to a principal of £100 (percent per annum)

	7%	8%	9%	10%
1 year	107 00	108 00	109 00	110 00
5 years	135 00	140 00	145 00	150 00
10 years	170 00	180 00	190 00	200 00
20 years	240 00	260 00	280 00	300 00
30 years	310 00	340 00	370 00	400 00
40 years	380 00	420 00	460 00	500 00
50 years	450 00	500 00	550 00	600 00

4.5%	5%	5.5%	6%	6.5%	7%
0.125	0.139	0.153	0.167	0.185	0.194
0.250	0.278	0.306	0.333	0.361	0.389
0.375	0.417	0.458	0.500	0.545	0.583
0.500	0.556	0.611	0.667	0.722	0.778
0.625	0.694	0.764	0.833	0.903	0.972
0.750	0.833	0.917	1.000	1.083	1.167
3.750	4.167	4.583	5.000	5.417	5.833
7.500	8.333	9.167	10.000	10.833	11.667
11.250	12.500	13.750	15.000	16.250	17.500
22.500	25.000	27.500	30.000	32.500	35.000
45.000	50.000	55.000	60.000	65.000	70.000

11%	12%	13%	14%	15%
111 00	112 00	113 00	114 00	115 00
155 00	160 00	165 00	170 00	175 00
210 00	220 00	230 00	240 00	250 00
320 00	340 00	360 00	380 00	400 00
430 00	460 00	490 00	520 00	550 00
540 00	580 00	620 00	660 00	700 00
650 00	700 00	750 00	800 00	850 00

Compound interest

The table below shows the compound interest paid (in pounds) on a principal of £100. The interest rate is in percent per annum.

Period	4%	5%	6%	7%
1 day	0.011	0.014	0.016	0.019
1 week	0.077	0.096	0.115	0.134
6 months	2.00	2.50	3.00	3.50
1 year	4.00	5.00	6.00	7.00
2 years	8.16	10.25	12.36	14.49
3 years	12.49	15.76	19.10	22.50
4 years	16.99	21.55	26.25	31.08
5 years	21.67	27.63	33.82	40.26
6 years	26.53	34.01	41.85	50.07
7 years	31.59	40.71	50.36	60.58
8 years	36.86	47.75	59.38	71.82
9 years	42.33	55.13	68.95	83.85
10 years	48.02	62.89	79.08	96.72

Comparing the two

Money grows much more quickly with compound interest than with simple interest. Compare, for example, the amount of time required for an amount of money to double itself with simple interest and with compound interest:

8%	9%	10%	12%	14%	16%
0.022	0.025	0.027	0.033	0.038	0.044
0.153	0.173	0.192	0.230	0.268	0.307
4.00	4.50	5.00	6.00	7.00	8.00
8.00	9.00	10.00	12.00	14.00	16.00
16.64	18.81	21.00	25.44	29.96	34.56
25.97	29.50	33.10	40.49	48.15	56.09
36.05	41.16	46.41	57.35	68.90	81.06
46.93	53.86	61.05	76.23	92.54	110.03
58.69	67.71	77.16	97.38	119.50	143.64
71.38	82.80	94.87	121.07	150.23	182.62
85.09	99.26	114.36	147.60	185.26	227.84
99.90	117.19	135.79	177.31	225.19	280.30
115.89	136.74	159.37	210.58	270.72	341.14

Rate	Simple	Compound
7%	14 yrs, 104 days	10 yrs, 89 days
10%	10 yrs	7 yrs, 100 days

2: Length and area

Formulas: length

Below are listed the multiplication/division factors for
converting units of length from imperial to metric, and
vice versa. Note that two kinds of factors are given:
quick, for an approximate conversion that can be made
without a calculator; and accurate, for an exact
conversion.

Milli-inches (mils) Micrometres (μm)		**Quick**	**Accurate**
mils ⟶ μm		× 25	× 25.4
μm ⟶ mils		÷ 25	× 0.0394
Inches (in) Millimetres (mm)			
in ⟶ mm		× 25	× 25.4
mm ⟶ in		÷ 25	× 0.0394
Inches (in) Centimetres (cm)			
in ⟶ cm		× 2.5	× 2.54
cm ⟶ in		÷ 2.5	× 0.394
Feet (ft) Metres (m)			
m ⟶ ft		× 3.3	× 3.281
ft ⟶ m		÷ 3.3	× 0.305
Yards (yd) Metres (m)			
m ⟶ yd		× 1	× 1.094
yd ⟶ m		÷ 1	× 0.914

Fathoms (fm) Metres (m)		**Quick**	**Accurate**
fm ➞ m		× 2	× 1.83
m ➞ fm		÷ 2	× 0.547

Chains (ch) Metres (m)			
ch ➞ m		× 20	× 20.108
m ➞ ch		÷ 20	× 0.0497

Furlongs (fur) Metres (m)			
fur ➞ m		× 200	× 201.17
m ➞ fur		÷ 200	× 0.005

Yards (yd) Kilometres (km)			
km ➞ yd		× 1000	× 1093.6
yd ➞ km		÷ 1000	× 0.00091

Miles (mi) Kilometres (km)			
mi ➞ km		× 1.5	× 1.609
km ➞ mi		÷ 1.5	× 0.621

Nautical miles (n mi) Miles (mi)			
n mi ➞ mi		× 1.2	× 1.151
mi ➞ n mi		÷ 1.2	× 0.869

Nautical miles (n mi) Kilometres (km)			
n mi ➞ km		× 2	× 1.852
km ➞ n mi		÷ 2	× 0.54

Conversion tables: length

The tables below can be used to convert units of length
from one measuring system to another. The first group
of tables converts imperial to metric; the second,
beginning on page 66, converts metric to imperial.

Milli-inches to Micrometres		Inches to Millimetres		Inches to Centimetres	
mils	µm	in	mm	in	cm
1	25.4	1	25.4	1	2.54
2	50.8	2	50.8	2	5.08
3	76.2	3	76.2	3	7.62
4	101.6	4	101.6	4	10.16
5	127.0	5	127.0	5	12.70
6	152.4	6	152.4	6	15.24
7	177.8	7	177.8	7	17.78
8	203.2	8	203.2	8	20.32
9	228.6	9	228.6	9	22.86
10	254.0	10	254.0	10	25.40
20	508.0	20	508.0	20	50.80
30	762.0	30	762.0	30	76.20
40	1016.0	40	1016.0	40	101.60
50	1270.0	50	1270.0	50	127.00
60	1524.0	60	1524.0	60	152.40
70	1778.0	70	1778.0	70	177.80
80	2032.0	80	2032.0	80	203.20
90	2286.0	90	2286.0	90	228.60
100	2540.0	100	2540.0	100	254.00

Feet to Metres		Yards to Metres		Fathoms to Metres	
ft	m	yd	m	fm	m
1	0.305	1	0.914	1	1.83
2	0.610	2	1.829	2	3.66
3	0.914	3	2.743	3	5.49
4	1.219	4	3.658	4	7.32
5	1.524	5	4.572	5	9.14
6	1.829	6	5.486	6	10.97
7	2.134	7	6.401	7	12.80
8	2.438	8	7.315	8	14.63
9	2.743	9	8.230	9	16.46
10	3.048	10	9.144	10	18.29
20	6.096	20	18.288	20	36.58
30	9.144	30	27.432	30	54.87
40	12.192	40	36.576	40	73.16
50	15.240	50	45.720	50	91.45
60	18.288	60	54.864	60	109.74
70	21.336	70	64.008	70	128.03
80	24.384	80	73.152	80	146.32
90	27.432	90	82.296	90	164.61
100	30.480	100	91.440	100	182.90

Imperial and metric units of length (continued)

Chains to Metres	
ch	m
1	20.108
2	40.216
3	60.324
4	80.432
5	100.540
6	120.648
7	140.756
8	160.864
9	180.972
10	201.080
20	402.160
30	603.240
40	804.320
50	1005.400
60	1206.480
70	1407.560
80	1608.640
90	1809.720
100	2010.800

Furlongs to Metres	
fur	m
1	201.17
2	402.34
3	603.50
4	804.67
5	1005.84
6	1207.01
7	1408.18
8	1609.34
9	1810.51
10	2011.68
20	4023.36
30	6035.04
40	8046.72
50	10 058.40
60	12 070.08
70	14 081.76
80	16 093.44
90	18 105.12
100	20 116.80

Yards to Kilometres	
yd	km
100	0.091
200	0.183
300	0.274
400	0.366
500	0.457
600	0.549
700	0.640
800	0.731
900	0.823
1000	0.914
2000	1.829
3000	2.743
4000	3.658
5000	4.572
6000	5.486
7000	6.401
8000	7.315
9000	8.230
10 000	9.144

Miles to Kilometres		Nautical miles to Miles		Nautical miles to Kilometres	
mi	km	n mi	mi	n mi	km
1	1.609	1	1.151	1	1.852
2	3.219	2	2.302	2	3.704
3	4.828	3	3.452	3	5.556
4	6.437	4	4.603	4	7.408
5	8.047	5	5.754	5	9.260
6	9.656	6	6.905	6	11.112
7	11.265	7	8.055	7	12.964
8	12.875	8	9.206	8	14.816
9	14.484	9	10.357	9	16.668
10	16.093	10	11.508	10	18.520
20	32.187	20	23.016	20	37.040
30	48.280	30	34.523	30	55.560
40	64.374	40	46.031	40	74.080
50	80.467	50	57.539	50	92.600
60	96.561	60	69.047	60	111.120
70	112.654	70	80.554	70	129.640
80	128.748	80	92.062	80	148.160
90	144.841	90	103.570	90	166.680
100	160.934	100	115.078	100	185.200

Imperial and metric units of length (continued)

Micrometres to Milli-inches		Millimetres to Inches		Centimetres to Inches	
µm	mils	mm	in	cm	in
1	0.039	1	0.039	1	0.394
2	0.079	2	0.079	2	0.787
3	0.118	3	0.118	3	1.181
4	0.157	4	0.157	4	1.575
5	0.197	5	0.197	5	1.969
6	0.236	6	0.236	6	2.362
7	0.276	7	0.276	7	2.756
8	0.315	8	0.315	8	3.150
9	0.354	9	0.354	9	3.543
10	0.394	10	0.394	10	3.937
20	0.787	20	0.787	20	7.874
30	1.181	30	1.181	30	11.811
40	1.575	40	1.575	40	15.748
50	1.969	50	1.969	50	19.685
60	2.362	60	2.362	60	23.622
70	2.756	70	2.756	70	27.559
80	3.150	80	3.150	80	31.496
90	3.543	90	3.543	90	35.433
100	3.937	100	3.937	100	39.370

Metres to Feet		Metres to Yards		Metres to Fathoms	
m	**ft**	**m**	**yd**	**m**	**fm**
1	3.281	1	1.094	1	0.547
2	6.562	2	2.187	2	1.093
3	9.843	3	3.281	3	1.640
4	13.123	4	4.374	4	2.187
5	16.404	5	5.468	5	2.734
6	19.685	6	6.562	6	3.280
7	22.966	7	7.655	7	3.827
8	26.247	8	8.749	8	4.374
9	29.528	9	9.843	9	4.921
10	32.808	10	10.936	10	5.467
20	65.617	20	21.872	20	10.935
30	98.425	30	32.808	30	16.402
40	131.234	40	43.745	40	21.870
50	164.042	50	54.681	50	27.337
60	196.850	60	65.617	60	32.805
70	229.659	70	76.553	70	38.272
80	262.467	80	87.489	80	43.740
90	295.276	90	98.425	90	49.207
100	328.084	100	109.361	100	54.674

Imperial and metric units of length (continued)

Metres to Chains		Metres to Furlongs		Kilometres to Yards	
m	ch	m	fur	km	yd
1	0.0497	1	0.005	1	1093.6
2	0.0994	2	0.010	2	2187.2
3	0.1491	3	0.015	3	3280.8
4	0.1989	4	0.020	4	4374.4
5	0.2487	5	0.025	5	5468.0
6	0.2983	6	0.030	6	6561.6
7	0.3481	7	0.035	7	7655.2
8	0.3979	8	0.040	8	8748.8
9	0.4476	9	0.045	9	9842.4
10	0.4973	10	0.050	10	10 936.0
20	0.9946	20	0.099	20	21 872.0
30	1.4919	30	0.149	30	32 808.0
40	1.9893	40	0.199	40	43 744.0
50	2.4866	50	0.249	50	54 680.0
60	2.9839	60	0.298	60	65 616.0
70	3.4812	70	0.348	70	76 552.0
80	3.9785	80	0.398	80	87 488.0
90	4.4758	90	0.447	90	98 424.0
100	4.9731	100	0.497	100	109 360.0

Kilometres to Miles		Miles to Nautical miles		Kilometres to Nautical miles	
km	mi	mi	n mi	km	n mi
1	0.621	1	0.869	1	0.54
2	1.243	2	1.738	2	1.08
3	1.864	3	2.607	3	1.62
4	2.485	4	3.476	4	2.16
5	3.107	5	4.349	5	2.70
6	3.728	6	5.214	6	3.24
7	4.350	7	6.083	7	3.78
8	4.971	8	6.952	8	4.32
9	5.592	9	7.821	9	4.86
10	6.214	10	8.690	10	5.40
20	12.427	20	17.380	20	10.80
30	18.641	30	26.069	30	16.20
40	24.855	40	34.759	40	21.60
50	31.069	50	43.449	50	27.00
60	37.282	60	52.139	60	32.40
70	43.496	70	60.828	70	37.80
80	49.710	80	69.518	80	43.20
90	55.923	90	78.208	90	48.60
100	62.137	100	86.900	100	54.00

Formulas: area
Below are listed the multiplication/division factors for
converting units of area from imperial to metric, and
vice versa. Note that two kinds of factors are given:
quick, for an approximate conversion that can be made
without a calculator; and accurate, for an exact
conversion.

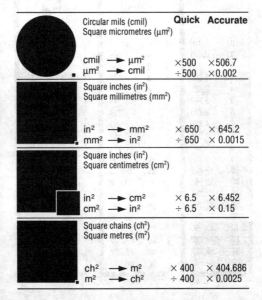

		Quick	**Accurate**
	Circular mils (cmil) Square micrometres (μm^2)		
	cmil $\longrightarrow$ μm^2	×500	×506.7
	μm^2 $\longrightarrow$ cmil	÷500	×0.002
	Square inches (in^2) Square millimetres (mm^2)		
	in^2 $\longrightarrow$ mm^2	× 650	× 645.2
	mm^2 $\longrightarrow$ in^2	÷ 650	× 0.0015
	Square inches (in^2) Square centimetres (cm^2)		
	in^2 $\longrightarrow$ cm^2	× 6.5	× 6.452
	cm^2 $\longrightarrow$ in^2	÷ 6.5	× 0.15
	Square chains (ch^2) Square metres (m^2)		
	ch^2 $\longrightarrow$ m^2	× 400	× 404.686
	m^2 $\longrightarrow$ ch^2	÷ 400	× 0.0025

	Quick	Accurate
Square miles (mi²)		
Square kilometres (km²)		
mi² → km²	× 2.5	× 2.590
km² → mi²	÷ 2.5	× 0.386
Square miles (mi²)		
Hectares (ha)		
mi² → ha	× 250	× 258.999
ha → mi²	÷ 250	× 0.0039
Hectares (ha)		
Acres		
ha → acre	× 2.5	× 2.471
acre → ha	÷ 2.5	× 0.405
Square metres (m²)		
Square yards (yd²)		
m² → yd²	× 1	× 1.196
yd² → m²	÷ 1	× 0.836
Square metres (m²)		
Square feet (ft²)		
m² → ft²	× 11	× 10.764
ft² → m²	÷ 11	× 0.093

Conversion tables: area

The tables below can be used to convert units of area from one measuring system to another. The first group of tables converts imperial to metric; the second, beginning on page 75, converts metric to imperial.

Circular mils to Square micrometres		Square inches to Square millimetres		Square inches to Square centimetres	
cmil	μm^2	in²	mm²	in²	cm²
1	506.7	1	645.2	1	6.452
2	1013.4	2	129.0	2	12.903
3	1520.1	3	193.6	3	19.355
4	2026.8	4	258.1	4	25.806
5	2533.5	5	322.6	5	32.258
6	3040.2	6	387.1	6	38.710
7	3546.9	7	451.6	7	45.161
8	4053.6	8	516.1	8	51.613
9	4560.3	9	580.6	9	58.064
10	5067.0	10	6452.0	10	64.516
20	10 134.0	20	1290.0	20	129.032
30	15 201.0	30	1936.0	30	193.548
40	20 268.0	40	2581.0	40	258.064
50	25 335.0	50	3226.0	50	322.580
60	30 402.0	60	3871.0	60	387.096
70	35 469.0	70	4516.0	70	451.612
80	40 536.0	80	5161.0	80	516.128
90	45 603.0	90	5806.0	90	580.644
100	50 670.0	100	64 520.0	100	645.160

Square feet to Square metres		Square yards to Square metres		Square chains to Square metres	
ft²	m²	yd²	m²	ch²	m²
1	0.093	1	0.836	1	404.686
2	0.186	2	1.672	2	809.372
3	0.279	3	2.508	3	1214.058
4	0.372	4	3.345	4	1618.744
5	0.465	5	4.181	5	2023.430
6	0.557	6	5.017	6	2428.116
7	0.650	7	5.853	7	2832.802
8	0.743	8	6.689	8	3237.488
9	0.836	9	7.525	9	3642.174
10	0.929	10	8.361	10	4046.860
20	1.858	20	16.723	20	8093.720
30	2.787	30	25.084	30	12 140.580
40	3.716	40	33.445	40	16 187.440
50	4.645	50	41.806	50	20 234.300
60	5.574	60	50.168	60	24 281.160
70	6.503	70	58.529	70	28 328.020
80	7.432	80	66.890	80	32 374.880
90	8.361	90	75.251	90	36 421.740
100	9.290	100	83.613	100	40 468.600

Imperial and metric units of area (continued)

Acres to Hectares		Square miles to Hectares		Square miles to Square kilometres	
acre	ha	mi²	ha	mi²	km²
1	0.405	1	258.999	1	2.590
2	0.809	2	517.998	2	5.180
3	1.214	3	776.997	3	7.770
4	1.619	4	1035.996	4	10.360
5	2.023	5	1294.995	5	12.950
6	2.428	6	1553.994	6	15.540
7	2.833	7	1812.993	7	18.130
8	3.237	8	2071.992	8	20.720
9	3.642	9	2330.991	9	23.310
10	4.047	10	2589.990	10	25.900
20	8.094	20	5179.980	20	51.800
30	12.141	30	7769.970	30	77.700
40	16.187	40	10 359.960	40	103.600
50	20.234	50	12 949.950	50	129.499
60	24.281	60	15 539.940	60	155.399
70	28.328	70	18 129.930	70	181.299
80	32.375	80	20 719.920	80	207.199
90	36.422	90	23 309.910	90	233.099
100	40.469	100	25 899.900	100	258.999

Square micrometres to Circular mils	
µm²	cmil
1	0.002
2	0.004
3	0.006
4	0.008
5	0.010
6	0.012
7	0.014
8	0.016
9	0.018
10	0.020
20	0.040
30	0.060
40	0.080
50	0.100
60	0.120
70	0.140
80	0.160
90	0.180
100	0.200

Square millimetres to Square inches	
mm²	in²
1	0.0015
2	0.0031
3	0.0047
4	0.0062
5	0.0078
6	0.0093
7	0.0109
8	0.0124
9	0.0140
10	0.0155
20	0.0310
30	0.0465
40	0.0620
50	0.0775
60	0.0930
70	0.1085
80	0.1240
90	0.1395
100	0.1550

Square centimetres to Square inches	
cm²	in²
1	0.155
2	0.310
3	0.465
4	0.620
5	0.775
6	0.930
7	1.085
8	1.240
9	1.395
10	1.550
20	3.100
30	4.650
40	6.200
50	7.750
60	9.300
70	10.850
80	12.400
90	13.950
100	15.500

Imperial and metric units of area (continued)

Square metres to Square feet		Square metres to Square yards		Square metres to Square chains	
m²	ft²	m²	yd²	m²	ch²
1	10.764	1	1.196	1	0.002
2	21.528	2	2.392	2	0.004
3	32.292	3	3.588	3	0.006
4	43.056	4	4.784	4	0.008
5	53.820	5	5.980	5	0.010
6	64.583	6	7.176	6	0.012
7	75.347	7	8.372	7	0.014
8	86.111	8	9.568	8	0.016
9	96.875	9	10.764	9	0.018
10	107.639	10	11.960	10	0.020
20	215.278	20	23.920	20	0.040
30	322.917	30	35.880	30	0.060
40	430.556	40	47.840	40	0.080
50	538.196	50	59.800	50	0.100
60	645.835	60	71.759	60	0.120
70	753.474	70	83.719	70	0.140
80	861.113	80	95.679	80	0.160
90	968.752	90	107.639	90	0.180
100	1076.391	100	119.599	100	0.200

Hectares to Acres		Hectares to Square miles		Square kilometres to Square miles	
ha	acre	ha	mi²	km²	mi²
1	2.471	1	0.003 86	1	0.386
2	4.942	2	0.007 72	2	0.772
3	7.413	3	0.011 58	3	1.158
4	9.884	4	0.015 44	4	1.544
5	12.355	5	0.019 31	5	1.931
6	14.826	6	0.023 17	6	2.317
7	17.297	7	0.027 03	7	2.703
8	19.768	8	0.030 89	8	3.089
9	22.239	9	0.034 75	9	3.475
10	24.711	10	0.038 61	10	3.861
20	49.421	20	0.077 22	20	7.722
30	74.132	30	0.115 83	30	11.583
40	98.842	40	0.154 44	40	15.444
50	123.553	50	0.193 05	50	19.305
60	148.263	60	0.231 66	60	23.166
70	172.974	70	0.270 27	70	27.027
80	197.684	80	0.308 88	80	30.888
90	222.395	90	0.347 49	90	34.749
100	247.105	100	0.386 10	100	38.610

Geometry of area
ABBREVIATIONS
a = length of top
b = length of base
h = perpendicular height
r = length of radius

$$\pi = 3.1416$$

Circle

$$\pi \times r^2$$

Rectangle

$$b \times h$$

Parallelogram

$$b \times h$$

Triangle

$$\frac{1}{2} \times b \times h$$

Trapezium

$$\frac{(a + b)\, h}{2}$$

Geometry of surface area

ABBREVIATIONS
b = breadth of base
h = perpendicular height
l = length of base
r = length of radius

$$\pi = 3.1416$$

	Cube $$h \times b \times 6$$
	Prism $$(b \times h) + (3 \times l \times b)$$
	Cylinder $$(2 \times \pi \times r \times l) + (2 \times \pi \times r^2)$$
	Pyramid $$(2 \times b \times h) + (b^2)$$
	Sphere $$4 \times \pi \times r^2$$

3: Volume

Formulas

Below are listed the multiplication/division factors for converting units of volume from one measuring system to another. Note that two kinds of factors are given: quick, for an approximate conversion that can be made without a calculator; and accurate, for an exact conversion.

		Quick	**Accurate**
1 1	UK gallons (gal) US fluid gallons (fl gal)		
	UK gal ⟶ US fl gal	× 1	× 1.201
	US fl gal ⟶ UK gal	÷ 1	× 0.833
1 1	UK quarts (qt) US fluid quarts (fl qt)		
	UK qt ⟶ US fl qt	× 1	× 1.201
	US fl qt ⟶ UK qt	÷ 1	× 0.833
1 1	UK pints (pt) US fluid pints (fl pt)		
	UK pt ⟶ US fl pt	× 1	× 1.201
	US fl pt ⟶ UK pt	÷ 1	× 0.833
1 1	UK fluid ounces (fl oz) US fluid ounces (fl oz)		
	UK fl oz ⟶ US fl oz	× 1	× 0.961
	US fl oz ⟶ UK fl oz	÷ 1	× 1.041
1 2	UK fluid ounces (fl oz) Cubic inches (in^3)		
	UK fl oz ⟶ in^3	× 2	× 1.734
	in^3 ⟶ UK fl oz	÷ 2	× 0.577

			Quick	**Accurate**
1 16	Cubic inches (in³) Cubic centimetres (cm³)	in³ → cm³	× 16	× 16.387
		cm³ → in³	÷ 16	× 0.061
1 28	UK fluid ounces (fl oz) Millilitres (ml)	UK fl oz → ml	× 28	× 28.413
		ml → UK fl oz	÷ 28	× 0.035
1 1	UK quarts (qt) Litres (l)	UK qt → l	× 1	× 1.137
		l → UK qt	÷ 1	× 0.880
1 4.5	UK gallons (gal) Litres (l)	UK gal → l	× 4.5	× 4.546
		l → UK gal	÷ 4.5	× 0.220
1 2	Litres (l) UK pints (pt)	l → UK pt	× 2	× 1.760
		UK pt → l	÷ 2	× 0.568
1 35	Cubic metres (m³) Cubic feet (ft³)	m³ → ft³	× 35	× 35.315
		ft³ → m³	÷ 35	× 0.028
1 1	Cubic metres (m³) Cubic yards (yd³)	m³ → yd³	× 1	× 1.308
		yd³ → m³	÷ 1	× 0.765

1 220

Cubic metres (m^3)
UK gallons (gal)

	Quick	**Accurate**
m^3 ⟶ UK gal	× 220	× 219.970
UK gal ⟶ m^3	÷ 220	× 0.005

1 30

US fluid ounces (fl oz)
Millilitres (ml)

US fl oz ⟶ ml	× 30	× 29.572
ml ⟶ US fl oz	÷ 30	× 0.034

1 4

US fluid gallons (fl gal)
Litres (l)

US fl gal ⟶ l	× 4	× 3.785
l ⟶ US fl gal	÷ 4	× 0.264

1 2

Litres (l)
US fluid pints (fl pt)

l ⟶ US fl pt	× 2	× 2.113
US fl pt ⟶ l	÷ 2	× 0.473

1 1

Litres (l)
US fluid quarts (fl qt)

l ⟶ US fl qt	× 1	× 1.056
US fl qt ⟶ l	÷ 1	× 0.947

1 264

Cubic metres (m^3)
US fluid gallons (fl gal)

m^3 ⟶ US fl gal	× 264	× 264.173
US fl gal ⟶ m^3	÷ 264	× 0.004

1 227

Cubic metres (m^3)
US dry gallons (dry gal)

m^3 ⟶ dry gal	× 227	× 227.020
dry gal ⟶ m^3	÷ 227	× 0.004

Conversion tables

The tables below can be used to convert units of volume from one measuring system to another. The first group of tables, beginning below, converts UK imperial to US imperial units; the second, beginning on page 85, converts US imperial to UK imperial units.

UK gallons to US fluid gallons		UK quarts to US fluid quarts	
UK gal	US fl gal	UK qt	US fl qt
1	1.201	1	1.201
2	2.402	2	2.402
3	3.603	3	3.603
4	4.804	4	4.804
5	6.005	5	6.005
6	7.206	6	7.206
7	8.407	7	8.407
8	9.608	8	9.608
9	10.809	9	10.809
10	12.010	10	12.010
20	24.020	20	24.020
30	36.030	30	36.030
40	48.040	40	48.040
50	60.050	50	60.050
60	72.060	60	72.060
70	84.070	70	84.070
80	96.080	80	96.080
90	108.090	90	108.090
100	120.100	100	120.100

UK imperial to US imperial conversions (continued)

UK pints to US fluid pints		UK fluid ounces to US fluid ounces	
UK pt	US fl pt	UK fl oz	US fl oz
1	1.201	1	0.961
2	2.402	2	1.922
3	3.603	3	2.882
4	4.804	4	3.843
5	6.005	5	4.804
6	7.206	6	5.765
7	8.407	7	6.726
8	9.608	8	7.686
9	10.809	9	8.647
10	12.010	10	9.608
20	24.020	20	19.216
30	36.030	30	28.824
40	48.040	40	38.432
50	60.050	50	48.040
60	72.060	60	57.648
70	84.070	70	67.256
80	96.080	80	76.864
90	108.090	90	86.472
100	120.100	100	96.080

US imperial to UK imperial conversions
The conversion tables below are used to convert US units of volume to metric units; tables beginning on page 95 convert metric unit to US.

US fluid gallons to UK gallons		US fluid quarts to UK quarts	
UK fl gal	UK gal	US fl qt	UK qt
1	0.833	1	0.833
2	1.665	2	1.665
3	2.498	3	2.498
4	3.331	4	3.331
5	4.164	5	4.164
6	4.998	6	4.996
7	5.829	7	5.829
8	6.662	8	6.662
9	7.494	9	7.494
10	8.327	10	8.327
20	16.654	20	16.654
30	24.981	30	24.981
40	33.308	40	33.308
50	41.635	50	41.635
60	49.962	60	49.962
70	58.289	70	58.289
80	66.616	80	66.616
90	74.943	90	74.943
100	83.270	100	83.270

US imperial to UK imperial conversions (continued)

US fluid pints to UK pints	
US fl pt	**UK pt**
1	0.833
2	1.665
3	2.498
4	3.331
5	4.164
6	4.996
7	5.829
8	6.662
9	7.494
10	8.327
20	16.654
30	24.981
40	33.308
50	41.635
60	49.962
70	58.289
80	66.616
90	74.943
100	83.270

US fluid ounces to UK fluid ounces	
US fl oz	**UK fl oz**
1	1.041
2	2.082
3	3.122
4	4.163
5	5.204
6	6.245
7	7.286
8	8.327
9	9.367
10	10.408
20	20.816
30	31.224
40	41.632
50	52.040
60	62.448
70	72.856
80	83.264
90	93.672
100	104.080

UK imperial to metric conversions

The conversion tables below are used to convert UK imperial units of volume to cubic units and metric units; tables beginning on page 90 convert metric units to UK imperial units.

UK fluid ounces to Cubic inches		Cubic inches to Cubic centimetres		Cubic feet to Cubic metres	
UK fl oz	in³	in³	cm³	ft³	m³
1	1.734	1	16.387	1	0.028
2	3.468	2	32.774	2	0.057
3	5.202	3	49.161	3	0.085
4	6.935	4	65.548	4	0.113
5	8.669	5	81.935	5	0.142
6	10.403	6	98.322	6	0.170
7	12.137	7	114.709	7	0.198
8	13.871	8	131.096	8	0.227
9	15.605	9	147.484	9	0.255
10	17.339	10	163.871	10	0.283
20	34.677	20	327.741	20	0.566
30	52.016	30	491.612	30	0.850
40	69.355	40	655.482	40	1.133
50	86.694	50	819.353	50	1.416
60	104.032	60	983.224	60	1.699
70	121.371	70	1147.094	70	1.982
80	138.710	80	1310.965	80	2.266
90	156.048	90	1474.835	90	2.549
100	173.387	100	1638.706	100	2.832

UK imperial to metric conversions (continued)

Cubic yards to Cubic metres		UK gallons to Cubic metres		UK gallons to Litres	
yd³	m³	UK gal	m³	UK gal	l
1	0.765	1	0.005	1	4.546
2	1.529	2	0.009	2	9.092
3	2.294	3	0.014	3	13.638
4	3.058	4	0.018	4	18.184
5	3.823	5	0.023	5	22.730
6	4.587	6	0.027	6	27.277
7	5.352	7	0.032	7	31.823
8	6.116	8	0.036	8	36.369
9	6.881	9	0.041	9	40.915
10	7.646	10	0.045	10	45.461
20	15.291	20	0.091	20	90.922
30	22.937	30	0.136	30	136.383
40	30.582	40	0.182	40	181.844
50	38.228	50	0.227	50	227.305
60	45.873	60	0.273	60	272.765
70	53.519	70	0.318	70	318.226
80	61.164	80	0.364	80	363.687
90	68.810	90	0.409	90	409.148
100	76.455	100	0.455	100	454.609

UK quarts to Litres		UK pints to Litres		UK fluid ounces to Millilitres	
UK qt	l	UK pt	l	UK fl oz	ml
1	1.137	1	0.568	1	28.413
2	2.273	2	1.137	2	56.826
3	3.410	3	1.705	3	85.239
4	4.546	4	2.273	4	113.652
5	5.683	5	2.841	5	142.065
6	6.819	6	3.410	6	170.478
7	7.956	7	3.978	7	198.891
8	9.092	8	4.546	8	227.305
9	10.229	9	5.114	9	255.718
10	11.365	10	5.683	10	284.131
20	22.730	20	11.365	20	568.261
30	34.096	30	17.048	30	852.392
40	45.461	40	22.730	40	1136.523
50	56.826	50	28.413	50	1420.654
60	68.191	60	34.096	60	1704.784
70	79.556	70	39.778	70	1988.915
80	90.922	80	45.461	80	2273.046
90	102.287	90	51.143	90	2557.177
100	113.652	100	56.826	100	2841.307

Metric to UK imperial conversions
The tables below convert metric units to UK imperial
units.

Millilitres to UK fluid ounces		Litres to UK pints		Litres to UK quarts	
ml	UK fl oz	l	UK pt	l	UK qt
1	0.035	1	1.760	1	0.880
2	0.070	2	3.520	2	1.760
3	0.106	3	5.279	3	2.640
4	0.141	4	7.039	4	3.520
5	0.176	5	8.799	5	4.399
6	0.211	6	10.559	6	5.279
7	0.246	7	12.318	7	6.159
8	0.282	8	14.078	8	7.039
9	0.317	9	15.838	9	7.919
10	0.352	10	17.598	10	8.799
20	0.704	20	35.195	20	17.598
30	1.056	30	52.793	30	26.396
40	1.408	40	70.390	40	35.195
50	1.760	50	87.988	50	43.994
60	2.112	60	105.585	60	52.793
70	2.464	70	123.183	70	61.591
80	2.816	80	140.780	80	70.390
90	3.168	90	158.378	90	79.189
100	3.520	100	175.975	100	87.988

Litres to UK gallons		Cubic metres to UK gallons		Cubic metres to Cubic feet	
l	UK gal	m³	UK gal	m³	ft³
1	0.220	1	219.970	1	35.315
2	0.440	2	439.940	2	70.629
3	0.660	3	659.909	3	105.944
4	0.880	4	879.879	4	141.259
5	1.100	5	1099.849	5	176.573
6	1.320	6	1319.818	6	211.888
7	1.540	7	1539.788	7	247.203
8	1.760	8	1759.757	8	282.517
9	1.980	9	1979.727	9	317.832
10	2.200	10	2199.697	10	353.147
20	4.399	20	4399.396	20	706.293
30	6.599	30	6599.093	30	1059.440
40	8.799	40	8798.789	40	1412.587
50	10.999	50	10 998.485	50	1765.734
60	13.198	60	13 198.181	60	2118.880
70	15.398	70	15 397.877	70	2472.027
80	17.598	80	17 597.573	80	2825.174
90	19.797	90	19 797.269	90	3178.320
100	21.997	100	21 996.965	100	3531.467

Metric to UK imperial conversions (continued)

Cubic metres to Cubic yards		Cubic centimetres to Cubic inches		Cubic inches to UK fluid ounces	
m³	yd³	cm³	in³	in³	UK fl oz
1	1.308	1	0.061	1	0.577
2	2.616	2	0.122	2	1.153
3	3.924	3	0.183	3	1.730
4	5.232	4	0.244	4	2.307
5	6.540	5	0.305	5	2.884
6	7.848	6	0.366	6	3.460
7	9.156	7	0.427	7	4.037
8	10.464	8	0.488	8	4.614
9	11.772	9	0.549	9	5.191
10	13.080	10	0.610	10	5.767
20	26.159	20	1.220	20	11.535
30	39.239	30	1.831	30	17.302
40	52.318	40	2.441	40	23.069
50	65.398	50	3.051	50	28.837
60	78.477	60	3.661	60	34.604
70	91.557	70	4.271	70	40.371
80	104.636	80	4.882	80	46.138
90	117.716	90	5.492	90	51.906
100	130.795	100	6.102	100	57.673

US imperial to metric conversions
The conversion tables below are used to convert US
imperial units of volume to metric units; tables
beginning on page 95 convert metric units to US
imperial units.

US fluid ounces to Millilitres US fl oz	ml	US fluid pints to Litres US fl pt	l	US fluid quarts to Litres US fl qt	l
1	29.572	1	0.473	1	0.947
2	59.145	2	0.946	2	1.894
3	88.717	3	1.420	3	2.840
4	118.289	4	1.893	4	3.787
5	147.862	5	2.366	5	4.734
6	177.434	6	2.839	6	5.681
7	207.006	7	3.312	7	6.628
8	236.579	8	3.785	8	7.575
9	266.152	9	4.259	9	8.521
10	295.724	10	4.732	10	9.468
20	591.447	20	9.464	20	18.937
30	887.171	30	14.195	30	28.405
40	1182.894	40	18.927	40	37.873
50	1478.618	50	23.659	50	47.341
60	1774.341	60	28.391	60	56.810
70	2070.065	70	33.123	70	66.278
80	2365.788	80	37.854	80	75.746
90	2661.512	90	42.586	90	85.215
100	2957.235	100	47.318	100	94.683

US imperial to metric conversions (continued)

US fluid gallons to Litres		US fluid gallons to Cubic metres		US dry gallons to Cubic metres	
US fl gal	l	US fl gal	m³	US dry gal	m³
1	3.785	1	0.004	1	0.004
2	7.571	2	0.008	2	0.009
3	11.356	3	0.011	3	0.013
4	15.141	4	0.015	4	0.018
5	18.927	5	0.019	5	0.022
6	22.712	6	0.023	6	0.026
7	26.497	7	0.026	7	0.031
8	30.282	8	0.030	8	0.035
9	34.068	9	0.034	9	0.040
10	37.853	10	0.038	10	0.044
20	75.706	20	0.076	20	0.088
30	113.559	30	0.114	30	0.132
40	151.412	40	0.151	40	0.176
50	189.265	50	0.189	50	0.220
60	227.118	60	0.227	60	0.264
70	264.971	70	0.265	70	0.308
80	302.824	80	0.303	80	0.352
90	340.677	90	0.341	90	0.396
100	378.530	100	0.379	100	0.440

Metric to US imperial conversions
The tables below convert metric units to US imperial units.

Millilitres to US fluid ounces		Litres to US fluid pints		Litres to US fluid quarts	
ml	US fl oz	l	US fl pt	l	US fl qt
1	0.034	1	2.113	1	1.056
2	0.068	2	4.227	2	2.112
3	0.101	3	6.340	3	3.168
4	0.135	4	8.454	4	4.225
5	0.169	5	10.567	5	5.281
6	0.203	6	12.680	6	6.337
7	0.237	7	14.794	7	7.393
8	0.271	8	16.907	8	8.449
9	0.304	9	19.020	9	9.505
10	0.338	10	21.134	10	10.562
20	0.676	20	42.268	20	21.123
30	1.014	30	63.401	30	31.685
40	1.353	40	84.535	40	42.246
50	1.691	50	105.669	50	52.808
60	2.029	60	126.803	60	63.369
70	2.367	70	147.937	70	73.931
80	2.705	80	169.070	80	84.493
90	3.043	90	190.204	90	95.054
100	3.382	100	211.338	100	105.616

Metric to US imperial conversions (continued)

Litres to US fluid gallons		Cubic metres to US fluid gallons		Cubic metres to US dry gallons	
l	US fl gal	m³	US fl gal	m³	US dry gal
1	0.264	1	264.173	1	227.020
2	0.528	2	528.346	2	454.041
3	0.793	3	792.519	3	681.061
4	1.057	4	1056.692	4	908.081
5	1.321	5	1320.865	5	1135.102
6	1.585	6	1585.038	6	1362.122
7	1.849	7	1849.211	7	1589.143
8	2.113	8	2113.385	8	1816.163
9	2.378	9	2377.558	9	2043.183
10	2.642	10	2641.731	10	2270.204
20	5.283	20	5283.462	20	4540.407
30	7.925	30	7925.192	30	6810.611
40	10.567	40	10 566.923	40	9080.814
50	13.209	50	13 208.653	50	11 351.018
60	15.850	60	15 850.383	60	13 621.221
70	18.492	70	18 492.115	70	15 891.425
80	21.134	80	21 133.846	80	18 161.628
90	23.775	90	23 775.578	90	20 431.832
100	26.417	100	26 417.308	100	22 702.036

Geometry of volume
ABBREVIATIONS
b = breadth of base
h = perpendicular height
l = length of base
r = length of radius

$\pi = 3.1416$

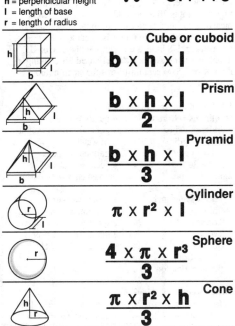

Cube or cuboid

$$b \times h \times l$$

Prism

$$\frac{b \times h \times l}{2}$$

Pyramid

$$\frac{b \times h \times l}{3}$$

Cylinder

$$\pi \times r^2 \times l$$

Sphere

$$\frac{4 \times \pi \times r^3}{3}$$

Cone

$$\frac{\pi \times r^2 \times h}{3}$$

Cooking measures

Although the names of the units are often the same, US measures are slightly different from imperial measures – for example, the US pint is 16 ounces, and the imperial pint is 20 ounces. US cooks use different measures for liquids and solids; in the imperial system used in the UK, a fluid ounce is equal to a dry ounce. On average, US units are roughly 4/5 the size of UK units. Metric measures are rarely used for cooking in the UK or US, except millilitres for small liquid amounts.

UK liquid and dry measures

60 minims = 1 dram	4 quarts = 1 gallon
8 drams = 1 fl oz	1 gallon = 10 lb (weight
5 fl oz = 1 gill	in water)
1 gill = 1/4 pint	2 gallons = 1 peck
1 pint = 20 fl oz	4 pecks = 1 bushel
2 pints = 1 quart	36 bushels = 1 chaldron

US liquid measures

60 minims = 1 fl dram
8 fl drams = 1 fl oz
4 fl oz = 1 gill
4 gills = 1 pint
2 pints = 1 quart
4 quarts = 1 gallon

US dry measures

1 dry pint = 1/2 dry quart
2 dry pints = 1 dry quart
8 dry quarts = 1 peck
4 pecks = 1 bushel

Water weights

1 fl oz water = 1 oz	1 quart water = 2 1/2 lb
1 pint water = 1 1/2 lb	1 gallon water = 10 lb

Handy measures

Object	Imperial	Metric
1 thimbleful	30 drops	2.5 ml
60 drops	1 teaspoon	5 ml
1 teaspoon	1 dram	5 ml
1 dessertspoon	2 drams	10 ml
1 tablespoon	4 drams	20 ml
2 tablespoons	1 fl oz	40 ml
1 wine glass	2 fl oz	100 ml
1 tea cup	5 fl oz (1 gill)	200 ml
1 mug	10 fl oz (1/2 pint)	400 ml

Beverage measures

Beer measures

1 nip = ¼ pint	1 kilderkin = 2 firkins
1 small = ½ pint	1 barrel = 2 kilderkins
1 large = 1 pint	1 hogshead = 1½ barrels
1 flagon = 1 quart	1 butt = 2 hogsheads
1 anker = 10 gallons	1 tun = 2 butts
1 firkin = 9 gallons	216 gallons

Handy measures
small jigger = 1 fl oz
small wine
   glass = 2 fl oz
cocktail glass = ¼ pint
sherry glass = ¼ pint
large wine
   glass = ¼ pint
tumbler = ½ pint

Wine measures
10 gallons = 1 anker
1 hogshead = 63 gallons
2 hogsheads = 1 pipe
2 pipes = 1 tun
1 puncheon = 84 gallons
1 butt
(sherry) = 110 gallons

US spirits measures
1 pony = ½ jigger
1 jigger = 1½ shot
1 shot = 1 fl oz
1 pint = 16 shots
1 fifth = 25.6 shots
         1.6 pints
         0.8 quart
         0.758 litre

1 quart = 32 shots
         1¼ fifths
1 magnum
of wine = 2 quarts
         2½ bottles

Champagne bottle sizes

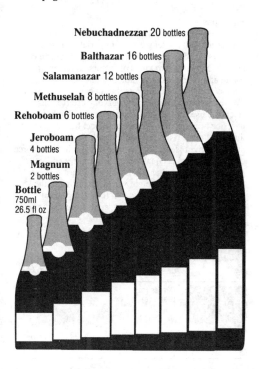

Nebuchadnezzar 20 bottles

Balthazar 16 bottles

Salamanazar 12 bottles

Methuselah 8 bottles

Rehoboam 6 bottles

Jeroboam
4 bottles

Magnum
2 bottles

Bottle
750ml
26.5 fl oz

4: Weight

Formulas

Below are listed the multiplication/division factors for converting units of length from imperial to metric, and vice versa, and from one unit to another in the same system. Note that two kinds of factors are given: quick, for an approximate conversion that can be made without a calculator; and accurate, for an exact conversion. The term "weight" differs in everyday use from its scientific use. In everyday terms, we use weight to describe how much substance an object has. In science, the term "mass" is used to describe this quantity of matter. Weight is used to describe the gravitational force on an object and is equal to its mass multiplied by the gravitational field strength. In scientific terms, mass remains constant but weight varies according to the strength of gravity. All units that follow are strictly units of mass rather than weight, apart from the pressure units kg/cm^2 and PSI.

		Quick	Accurate
Grains (gr) Grams (g)			
g ⟶ gr		× 15	× 15.432
gr ⟶ g		÷ 15	× 0.065
Ounces (oz) Grams (g)			
oz ⟶ g		× 28	× 28.349
g ⟶ oz		÷ 28	× 0.035

		Quick	**Accurate**
Ounces troy (oz tr) Grams (g)			
oz tr ⟶ g		× 31	× 31.103
g ⟶ oz tr		÷ 31	× 0.032
Stones (st) Kilograms (kg)			
st ⟶ kg		× 6	× 6.350
kg ⟶ st		÷ 6	× 0.157
Long tons (l t) Tonnes (t)			
l t ⟶ t		× 1	× 1.016
t ⟶ l t		÷ 1	× 0.984
Kilograms (kg) Pounds (lb)			
kg ⟶ lb		× 2	× 2.205
lb ⟶ kg		÷ 2	× 0.454
Kilograms per square centimetre (kg/cm²) Pounds per square inch (PSI)			
kg/cm² ⟶ PSI		× 14	× 14.223
PSI ⟶ kg/cm²		÷ 14	× 0.070
Tonnes (t) Short tons (sh t)			
t ⟶ sh t		× 1	× 1.102
sh t ⟶ t		÷ 1	× 0.907
Ounces troy (oz tr) Ounces (oz)			
oz tr ⟶ oz		× 1	× 1.097
oz ⟶ oz tr		÷ 1	× 0.911

Conversion tables

The tables below can be used to convert units of weight from one measuring system to another. The units included in the tables are UK imperial, US imperial troy, and metric.

Grains to Grams		Ounces to Grams		Ounces troy to Grams	
gr	g	oz	g	oz tr	g
1	0.065	1	28.349	1	31.103
2	0.130	2	56.699	2	62.207
3	0.194	3	85.048	3	93.310
4	0.259	4	113.398	4	124.414
5	0.324	5	141.747	5	155.517
6	0.389	6	170.097	6	186.621
7	0.454	7	198.446	7	217.724
8	0.518	8	226.796	8	248.829
9	0.583	9	255.145	9	279.931
10	0.648	10	283.495	10	311.035
20	1.296	20	566.990	20	622.070
30	1.944	30	850.485	30	933.104
40	2.592	40	1133.980	40	1244.139
50	3.240	50	1417.475	50	1555.174
60	3.888	60	1700.970	60	1866.209
70	4.536	70	1984.465	70	2177.243
80	5.184	80	2267.960	80	2488.278
90	5.832	90	2551.455	90	2799.313
100	6.480	100	2834.900	100	3110.348

Pounds to Kilograms	
lb	kg
1	0.454
2	0.907
3	1.361
4	1.814
5	2.268
6	2.722
7	3.175
8	3.629
9	4.082
10	4.536
20	9.072
30	13.608
40	18.144
50	22.680
60	27.216
70	31.751
80	36.287
90	40.823
100	45.359

Pounds per square inch to Kilograms per square centimetre	
PSI	kg/cm^2
10	0.703
15	1.055
20	1.406
22	1.547
24	1.687
26	1.828
28	1.986
30	2.109
32	2.250
34	2.390
36	2.531
38	2.671
40	2.812
45	3.164
50	3.515

Stones to Kilograms	
st	kg
1	6.350
2	12.700
3	19.050
4	25.401
5	31.751
6	38.101
7	44.452
8	50.802
9	57.152
10	63.502
20	127.006
30	190.509
40	254.012
50	317.515
60	381.018
70	444.521
80	508.023
90	571.526
100	635.029

Imperial and metric units of weight (continued)

Short tons to Tonnes		Long tons to Tonnes		Grams to Grains	
sh t	t	l t	t	g	gr
1	0.907	1	1.016	1	15.432
2	1.814	2	2.032	2	30.865
3	2.721	3	3.048	3	46.297
4	3.628	4	4.064	4	61.729
5	4.535	5	5.080	5	77.162
6	5.443	6	6.096	6	92.594
7	6.350	7	7.112	7	108.027
8	7.257	8	8.128	8	123.459
9	8.164	9	9.144	9	138.891
10	9.071	10	10.160	10	154.324
20	18.143	20	20.320	20	308.647
30	27.215	30	30.481	30	462.971
40	36.287	40	40.641	40	617.294
50	45.359	50	50.802	50	771.618
60	54.431	60	60.962	60	925.942
70	63.502	70	71.123	70	1080.265
80	72.574	80	81.283	80	1234.589
90	81.646	90	91.444	90	1388.912
100	90.718	100	101.604	100	1543.236

Grams to Ounces		Grams to Ounces troy		Kilograms to Pounds	
g	oz	g	oz tr	kg	lb
1	0.035	1	0.032	1	2.205
2	0.071	2	0.064	2	4.409
3	0.106	3	0.096	3	6.614
4	0.141	4	0.129	4	8.818
5	0.176	5	0.161	5	11.023
6	0.212	6	0.193	6	13.228
7	0.247	7	0.225	7	15.432
8	0.282	8	0.257	8	17.637
9	0.317	9	0.289	9	19.842
10	0.353	10	0.322	10	22.046
20	0.705	20	0.643	20	44.092
30	1.058	30	0.965	30	66.139
40	1.411	40	1.286	40	88.185
50	1.764	50	1.608	50	110.231
60	2.116	60	1.929	60	132.277
70	2.469	70	2.251	70	154.324
80	2.822	80	2.572	80	176.370
90	3.175	90	2.894	90	198.416
100	3.527	100	3.215	100	220.462

Imperial and metric units of weight (continued)

Kilograms per square centimetre to Pounds per square inch	
kg/cm²	PSI
0.6	8.534
0.8	11.378
1.0	14.223
1.2	17.068
1.4	19.912
1.6	22.757
1.8	25.601
2.0	28.446
2.2	31.291
2.4	34.135
2.6	36.980
2.8	39.824
3.0	42.669
3.2	45.514
3.5	49.781

Kilograms to Stones	
kg	st
1	0.157
2	0.315
3	0.472
4	0.630
5	0.787
6	0.945
7	1.102
8	1.260
9	1.417
10	1.574
20	3.149
30	4.724
40	6.299
50	7.874
60	9.448
70	11.023
80	12.598
90	14.173
100	15.747

Tonnes to Short tons	
t	sh t
1	1.102
2	2.205
3	3.307
4	4.409
5	5.512
6	6.614
7	7.716
8	8.818
9	9.921
10	11.023
20	22.046
30	33.069
40	44.092
50	55.116
60	66.139
70	77.162
80	88.185
90	99.208
100	110.231

Tonnes to Long tons		Ounces to Ounces troy		Ounces troy to Ounces	
t	l t	oz	oz tr	oz tr	oz
1	0.984	1	0.911	1	1.097
2	1.968	2	1.823	2	2.194
3	2.953	3	2.734	3	3.291
4	3.937	4	3.646	4	4.389
5	4.921	5	4.557	5	5.486
6	5.905	6	5.468	6	6.583
7	6.889	7	6.380	7	7.680
8	7.874	8	7.291	8	8.777
9	8.858	9	8.203	9	9.874
10	9.842	10	9.114	10	10.971
20	19.684	20	18.229	20	21.943
30	29.526	30	27.344	30	32.914
40	39.368	40	36.458	40	43.886
50	49.211	50	45.573	50	54.857
60	59.052	60	54.687	60	65.828
70	68.894	70	63.802	70	76.800
80	78.737	80	72.917	80	87.771
90	88.579	90	82.031	90	98.743
100	98.421	100	91.146	100	109.714

Periodic table

The periodic table is a means of classifying and
comparing chemical elements. Substances as different
as hydrogen, calcium and gold are all elements; each
has distinctive properties and cannot be split chemically
into a simpler form.

The table groups elements into seven rows or periods.
Elements in the vertical columns, or groups, have
similar properties. For example, the first element in any
period (called an alkali metal) is reactive; while
the last element (a noble, or inert, gas) is almost
totally non-reactive.

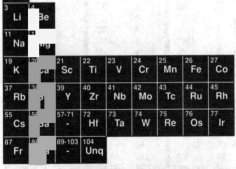

The elements are listed in the table in order of their atomic numbers, from 1 to 104 (appearing in the upper left-hand corner of each box). The atomic number represents the number of protons the element has in its nucleus.

The two bottom rows are the lanthanides (57–71) and the actinides (89–103). These are separate because they have such similar properties that they fit the space of only two elements in the main table.

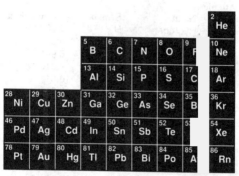

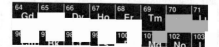

Chemical elements

On the following pages, the elements are listed in three separate ways: **1** by atomic number; **2** by element name; and **3** by letter symbol. Each listing includes the atomic number, element name, symbol, and atomic weight (or relative atomic mass) of each element.

* Indicates atomic weight of the isotope with the longest known half-life.

1 BY ATOMIC NUMBER

Atomic No.	Name	Symbol	Atomic weight
1	Hydrogen	H	1.007 9
2	Helium	He	4.002 6
3	Lithium	Li	6.941
4	Beryllium	Be	9.012 18
5	Boron	B	10.81
6	Carbon	C	12.011
7	Nitrogen	N	14.006 7
8	Oxygen	O	15.999 4
9	Fluorine	F	18.998 4
10	Neon	Ne	20.179
11	Sodium	Na	22.989 77
12	Magnesium	Mg	24.305
13	Aluminium	Al	26.981 54
14	Silicon	Si	28.085 5
15	Phosphorus	P	30.973 76
16	Sulphur	S	32.064
17	Chlorine	Cl	35.453
18	Argon	Ar	39.948
19	Potassium	K	39.098 3

Atomic No.	Name	Symbol	Atomic weight
20	Calcium	Ca	40.08
21	Scandium	Sc	44.955 9
22	Titanium	Ti	47.9
23	Vanadium	V	50.941 4
24	Chromium	Cr	51.996
25	Manganese	Mn	54.938
26	Iron	Fe	55.847
27	Cobalt	Co	58.933 2
28	Nickel	Ni	58.71
29	Copper	Cu	63.546
30	Zinc	Zn	65.381
31	Gallium	Ga	69.72
32	Germanium	Ge	72.59
33	Arsenic	As	74.921 6
34	Selenium	Se	78.96
35	Bromine	Br	79.904
36	Krypton	Kr	83.8
37	Rubidium	Rb	85.467 8
38	Strontium	Sr	87.62
39	Yttrium	Y	88.905 9
40	Zirconium	Zr	91.22
41	Niobium	Nb	92.906 4
42	Molybdenum	Mo	95.94
43	Technetium	Tc	96.906 4*
44	Ruthenium	Ru	101.07
45	Rhodium	Rh	102.905 5
46	Palladium	Pd	106.4

Atomic No.	Name	Symbol	Atomic weight
47	Silver	Ag	107.868
48	Cadmium	Cd	112.41
49	Indium	In	114.82
50	Tin	Sn	118.69
51	Antimony	Sb	121.75
52	Tellurium	Te	127.6
53	Iodine	I	126.904 5
54	Xenon	Xe	131.3
55	Caesium	Cs	132.905 4
56	Barium	Ba	137.33
57	Lanthanum	La	138.905 5
58	Caerium	Ce	140.12
59	Praseodymium	Pr	140.907 7
60	Neodymium	Nd	144.24
61	Promethium	Pm	144.912 8*
62	Samarium	Sm	150.35
63	Europium	Eu	151.96
64	Galolinium	Gd	157.25
65	Terbium	Tb	158.925 4
66	Dysprosium	Dy	162.5
67	Holmium	Ho	164.930 4
68	Erbium	Er	167.26
69	Thulium	Tm	168.934 2
70	Ytterbium	Yb	173.04
71	Lutetium	Lu	174.97
72	Hafnium	Hf	178.49
73	Tantalum	Ta	180.947 9
74	Tungsten	W	183.85

Atomic No.	Name	Symbol	Atomic weight
75	Rhenium	Re	186.207
76	Osmium	Os	190.2
77	Iridium	Ir	192.22
78	Platinum	Pt	195.09
79	Gold	Au	196.966 5
80	Mercury	Hg	200.59
81	Thallium	Tl	204.37
82	Lead	Pb	207.19
83	Bismuth	Bi	208.980 4
84	Polonium	Po	208.982 4*
85	Astatine	At	209.987 0*
86	Radon	Rn	222.017 6*
87	Francium	Fr	223.019 7*
88	Radium	Ra	226.025 4*
89	Actinium	Ac	227.027 8*
90	Thorium	Th	232.038 1
91	Protoactinium	Pa	231.035 9
92	Uranium	U	238.029*
93	Neptunium	Np	237.048 2*
94	Plutonium	Pu	244.064 2*
95	Americium	Am	243.061 4*
96	Curium	Cm	247.070 3*
97	Berkelium	Bk	247.070 3*
98	Californium	Cf	251.079 6*
99	Einsteinium	Es	254.088 0*
100	Fermium	Fm	257.095 1*
101	Mendelevium	Md	258.099*
102	Nobelium	No	259.101*

Atomic No.	Name	Symbol	Atomic weight
103	Lawrencium	Lr	260.105*
104	Unnilquadium	Unq	no data

2 BY ELEMENT NAME

Name	Atomic No.	Symbol	Atomic weight
Actinium	89	Ac	227.027 8*
Aluminium	13	Al	26.981 54
Americium	95	Am	243.061 4*
Antimony	51	Sb	121.75
Argon	18	Ar	39.948
Arsenic	33	As	74.921 6
Astatine	85	At	209.987 0*
Barium	56	Ba	137.33
Berkelium	97	Bk	247.070 3*
Beryllium	4	Be	9.012 18
Bismuth	83	Bi	208.980 4
Boron	5	B	10.81
Bromine	35	Br	79.904
Cadmium	48	Cd	112.41
Caesium	55	Cs	132.905 4
Calcium	20	Ca	40.08
Californium	98	Cf	251.079 6*
Carbon	6	C	12.011
Cerium	58	Ce	140.12
Chlorine	17	Cl	35.453
Chromium	24	Cr	51.996

Name	Atomic No.	Symbol	Atomic weight
Cobalt	27	Co	58.933 2
Copper	29	Cu	63.546
Curium	96	Cm	247.703*
Dysprosium	66	Dy	162.5
Einsteinium	99	Es	254.088 0*
Erbium	68	Er	167.26
Europium	63	Eu	151.96
Fermium	100	Fm	257.095 1*
Fluorine	9	F	18.998 4
Francium	87	Fr	223.019 7*
Gallium	31	Ga	69.72
Galolinium	64	Gd	157.25
Germanium	32	Ge	72.59
Gold	79	Au	196.966 5
Hafnium	72	Hf	178.49
Helium	2	He	4.002 6
Holmium	67	Ho	164.930 4
Hydrogen	1	H	1.007 9
Iodine	53	I	126.904 5
Indium	49	In	114.82
Iridium	77	Ir	192.22
Iron	26	Fe	55.847
Krypton	36	Kr	83.8
Lanthanum	57	La	138.905 5
Lawrencium	103	Lr	260.105*
Lead	82	Pb	207.19
Lithium	3	Li	6.941

Name	Atomic No.	Symbol	Atomic weight
Lutetium	71	Lu	174.97
Magnesium	12	Mg	24.305
Manganese	25	Mn	54.938
Mendelevium	101	Md	258.099*
Mercury	80	Hg	200.59
Molybdenum	42	Mo	95.94
Neodymium	60	Nd	144.24
Neon	10	Ne	20.179
Neptunium	93	Np	237.048 2*
Nickel	28	Ni	58.71
Niobium	41	Nb	92.906 4
Nitrogen	7	N	14.006 7
Nobelium	102	No	259.101*
Oxygen	8	O	15.999 4
Osmium	76	Os	190.2
Palladium	46	Pd	106.4
Phosphorus	15	P	30.973 76
Platinum	78	Pt	195.09
Plutonium	94	Pu	244.064 2*
Polonium	84	Po	208.982 4*
Potassium	19	K	39.098 3
Praseodymium	59	Pr	140.907 7
Promethium	61	Pm	144.912 8*
Protoactinium	91	Pa	231.035 9
Radium	88	Ra	226.0254*
Radon	86	Rn	222.017 6*
Rhenium	75	Re	186.207

Name	Atomic No.	Symbol	Atomic weight
Rhodium	45	Rh	102.905 5
Rubidium	37	Rb	85.467 8
Ruthenium	44	Ru	101.07
Samarium	62	Sm	150.35
Scandium	21	Sc	44.955 9
Selenium	34	Se	78.96
Sodium	11	Na	22.989 77
Silicon	14	Si	28.085 5
Silver	47	Ag	107.868
Strontium	38	Sr	87.62
Sulphur	16	S	32.064
Tantalum	73	Ta	180.947 9
Technetium	43	Tc	96.906 4*
Tellurium	52	Te	127.6
Terbium	65	Tb	158.925 4
Thallium	81	Tl	204.37
Thorium	90	Th	232.038 1
Thulium	69	Tm	168.934 2
Tin	50	Sn	118.69
Titanium	22	Ti	47.9
Tungsten	74	W	183.85
Unnilquadium	104	Unq	no data
Uranium	92	U	238.029*
Vanadium	23	V	50.941 4
Xenon	54	Xe	131.3
Ytterbium	70	Yb	173.04
Yttrium	39	Y	88.905 9

Name	Atomic No.	Symbol	Atomic weight
Zinc	30	Zn	65.381
Zirconium	40	Zr	91.22

3 BY LETTER SYMBOL

Symbol	Atomic No.	Name	Atomic weight
Ac	89	Actinium	227.027 8*
Ag	47	Silver	107.868
Al	13	Aluminium	26.981 54
Am	95	Americium	243.061 4*
Ar	18	Argon	39.948
As	33	Arsenic	74.921 6
At	85	Astatine	209.987 0*
Au	79	Gold	196.966 5
B	5	Boron	10.81
Ba	56	Barium	137.33
Be	4	Beryllium	9.012 18
Bk	97	Berkelium	247.070 3*
Bi	83	Bismuth	208.980 4
Br	35	Bromine	79.904
C	6	Carbon	12.011
Ca	20	Calcium	40.08
Cd	48	Cadmium	112.41
Ce	58	Cerium	140.12
Cf	98	Californium	251.079 6*
Cl	17	Chlorine	35.453
Cm	96	Curium	247.070 3*
Co	27	Cobalt	58.933 2

Symbol	Atomic No.	Name	Atomic weight
Cr	24	Chromium	51.996
Cs	55	Caesium	132.905 4
Cu	29	Copper	63.546
Dy	66	Dysprosium	162.5
Er	68	Erbium	167.26
Es	99	Einsteinium	254.088*
Eu	63	Europium	151.96
F	9	Fluorine	18.998 4
Fe	26	Iron	55.847
Fm	100	Fermium	257.095 1*
Fr	87	Francium	223.019 7*
Ga	31	Gallium	69.72
Gd	64	Galolinium	157.25
Ge	32	Germanium	72.59
H	1	Hydrogen	1.007 9
He	2	Helium	4.002 6
Hf	72	Hafnium	178.49
Hg	80	Mercury	200.59
Ho	67	Holmium	164.930 4
I	53	Iodine	126.904 5
In	49	Indium	114.82
Ir	77	Iridium	192.22
K	19	Potassium	39.098 3
Kr	36	Krypton	83.8
La	57	Lanthanum	138.905 5
Li	3	Lithium	6.941
Lr	103	Lawrencium	260.105*
Lu	71	Lutetium	174.97

Symbol	Atomic No.	Name	Atomic weight
Md	101	Mendelevium	258.099*
Mg	12	Magnesium	24.305
Mn	25	Manganese	54.938
Mo	42	Molybdenum	95.94
N	7	Nitrogen	14.006 7
Na	11	Sodium	22.989 77
Nb	41	Niobium	92.906 4
Nd	60	Neodymium	144.24
Ne	10	Neon	20.179
Ni	28	Nickel	58.71
No	102	Nobelium	259.101*
Np	93	Neptunium	237.048 2*
O	8	Oxygen	15.999 4
Os	76	Osmium	190.2
P	15	Phosphorus	30.973 76
Pa	91	Protoactinium	231.035 9
Pb	82	Lead	207.19
Pd	46	Palladium	106.4
Pm	61	Promethium	144.912 8*
Po	84	Polonium	208.982 4*
Pr	59	Praseodymium	140.907 7
Pt	78	Platinum	195.09
Pu	94	Plutonium	244.064 2*
Ra	88	Radium	226.025 4*
Rb	37	Rubidium	85.467 8
Re	75	Rhenium	186.207
Rh	45	Rhodium	102.905 5
Rn	86	Radon	222.017 6*

Symbol	Atomic No.	Name	Atomic weight
Ru	44	Ruthenium	101.07
S	16	Sulphur	32.064
Sb	51	Antimony	121.75
Sc	21	Scandium	44.955 9
Se	34	Selenium	78.96
Si	14	Silicon	28.085 5
Sm	62	Samarium	150.35
Sn	50	Tin	118.69
Sr	38	Strontium	87.62
Ta	73	Tantalum	180.947 9
Tb	65	Terbium	158.925 4
Tc	43	Technetium	96.906 4*
Te	52	Tellurium	127.6
Th	90	Thorium	232.038 1
Ti	22	Titanium	47.9
Tl	81	Thallium	204.37
Tm	69	Thulium	168.934 2
U	92	Uranium	238.029*
Unq	104	Unnilquadium	
V	23	Vanadium	50.941 4
W	74	Tungsten	183.85
Xe	54	Xenon	131.3
Y	39	Yttrium	88.905 9
Yb	70	Ytterbium	173.04
Zn	30	Zinc	65.381
Zr	40	Zirconium	91.22

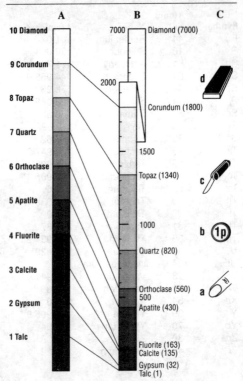

	A	B	C
10 Diamond		7000 — Diamond (7000)	
9 Corundum		2000	
8 Topaz		Corundum (1800)	d
7 Quartz		1500	
6 Orthoclase		Topaz (1340)	c
5 Apatite		1000	
4 Fluorite		Quartz (820)	b (1p)
3 Calcite		Orthoclase (560)	
2 Gypsum		500 — Apatite (430)	a
1 Talc		Fluorite (163) Calcite (135) Gypsum (32) Talc (1)	

Scales of hardness

Solids vary in their degree of hardness, which indicates their resistance to being scratched or cut.

A Mohs' scale

Mohs' scale is used to measure the relative hardness of minerals. The framework uses the 10 minerals – talc to diamond – shown in the scale. Each of these minerals is assigned a numerical value from 1 to 10: the higher the number, the harder the mineral.

Order is determined by the ability of a mineral to scratch all those that have a lower number and to be scratched by those with a higher number. Once this is established, it is possible to place all other minerals on the scale by means of the same scratching procedure.

B Knoop scale

Another system of measuring the hardness of minerals is the Knoop scale. The Knoop scale gives absolute rather than relative measurements. Readings on this scale are made by measuring the size of the indentation made by a diamond-shaped device dropped on the material.

Again, the higher the number the harder the substance, but the intervals between minerals and levels of hardness differ greatly from scale to scale. Minerals with values between 1 and 7 on Mohs' scale fall below 1000 on the Knoop scale, and between 8 and 9 fall below 2000, but diamond falls at 7000.

C Common-object scale

A simple way of measuring hardness uses common objects, whose hardness on the Mohs' scale is known:

a) fingernail (2–2.5 Mohs')   c) knife blade (5–6)

b) penny (4)   d) knife sharpener (8–9)

5: Energy

Formulas
Below are listed the multiplication/division factors for converting units of energy from imperial to metric, and vice versa. Note that two kinds of factors are given: quick, for an approximate conversion that can be made without a calculator; and accurate, for an exact conversion.

		Quick	**Accurate**
	Kilowatts (kW) Horsepower (hp)		
	kW ⟶ hp	× 1.5	× 1.341
	hp ⟶ kW	÷ 1.5	× 0.746
	Calories (cal) Joules (J)		
	cal ⟶ J	× 4	× 4.187
	J ⟶ cal	÷ 4	× 0.239
	Kilocalories (kcal) Kilojoules (kJ)		
	kcal ⟶ kJ	× 4	× 4.187
	kJ ⟶ kcal	÷ 4	× 0.239

Conversion tables

The tables below can be used to convert units of energy from metric to imperial systems, and vice versa.

Horsepower to Kilowatts		Kilowatts to Horsepower	
hp	**kW**	**kW**	**hp**
1	0.746	1	1.341
2	1.491	2	2.682
3	2.237	3	4.023
4	2.983	4	5.364
5	3.729	5	6.705
6	4.474	6	8.046
7	5.220	7	9.387
8	5.966	8	10.728
9	6.711	9	12.069
10	7.457	10	13.410
20	14.914	20	26.820
30	22.371	30	40.231
40	29.828	40	53.641
50	37.285	50	67.051
60	44.742	60	80.461
70	52.199	70	93.871
80	59.656	80	107.280
90	67.113	90	120.690
100	74.570	100	134.100

Metric units of energy

Joules to Calories international		Kilojoules to Kilocalories international	
J	cal	kJ	kcal
1	0.239	1	0.239
2	0.478	2	0.478
3	0.716	3	0.716
4	0.955	4	0.955
5	1.194	5	1.194
6	1.433	6	1.433
7	1.672	7	1.672
8	1.911	8	1.911
9	2.150	9	2.150
10	2.388	10	2.388
20	4.777	20	4.777
30	7.165	30	7.165
40	9.554	40	9.554
50	11.942	50	11.942
60	14.330	60	14.330
70	16.719	70	16.719
80	19.108	80	19.108
90	21.496	90	21.496
100	23.885	100	23.885

Calories international to Joules	
cal	J
1	4.187
2	8.374
3	12.560
4	16.747
5	20.934
6	25.121
7	29.308
8	33.494
9	37.681
10	41.868
20	83.736
30	125.604
40	167.472
50	209.340
60	251.208
70	293.076
80	334.944
90	376.812
100	418.680

Kilocalories international to Kilojoules	
kcal	kJ
1	4.187
2	8.374
3	12.560
4	16.747
5	20.934
6	25.121
7	29.308
8	33.494
9	37.681
10	41.868
20	83.736
30	125.604
40	167.472
50	209.340
60	251.208
70	293.076
80	334.944
90	376.812
100	418.680

Electromagnetic spectrum

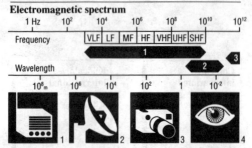

Measuring energy

Light and radio waves, X-rays, and other forms of
energy are transmitted through space as
electromagnetic waves. These waves have alternating
high and low points – crests and troughs – like actual
waves. The distance between wave crests is called the
wavelength; this is measured in metres. Frequency
refers to the number of waves per second; this is
measured in hertz (Hz).

Above is an electromagnetic spectrum, showing the
different forms of energy in order of frequency and
wavelength. The top part of the diagram shows the
frequency in hertz; the lower part measures the
wavelength in metres.

1 Radio waves

These waves transmit television and radio signals. This
section of the spectrum is divided into bands, from
VLF (very low frequency) – used for time signals – to
SHF (super-high frequency) – used for space and
satellite communication.

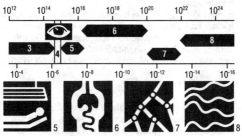

2 Radar and microwaves
Radar bounces waves off objects, allowing unseen objects to be seen; microwaves can cook food quickly.

3 Infrared waves
These waves are emitted by all hot objects.

4 Visible light
The band of visible light from red to violet.

5 Ultraviolet light
In small amounts, these waves produce vitamin D and cause skin to tan; in larger amounts they can damage living cells.

6 X-rays
Used to photograph internal structures of bodies.

7 Gamma rays
Emitted during the decay of some radioisotopes, these waves can be very damaging to the body.

8 Cosmic rays
Caused by nuclear explosions and reactions in space, nearly all of these waves are absorbed by the Earth's atmosphere.

Earthquakes

Earthquake magnitude is measured in units on the Richter scale, which measures the amount of energy released. Each year there are more than 300 000 earth tremors with Richter magnitudes of 2 to 2.9. An earthquake of 8.5 or higher occurs about every 5 to 10 years.

Intensity

The intensity of an earthquake is measured on the Mercalli scale; the numbers refer to an earthquake's effect at a specific place on the Earth's surface.

Below are listed numbers on the Mercalli scale and the characteristics of each.

No.	Characteristic
I	instrumental (detected only by seismograph)
II	feeble (noticed only by people at rest)
III	slight (similar to vibrations from a passing truck)
IV	moderate (felt indoors, parked cars rock)
V	rather strong (felt generally, waking sleepers)
VI	strong (trees sway, some damage)
VII	very strong (general alarm, walls crack)
VIII	destructive (walls collapse)
IX	ruinous (some houses collapse, ground cracks)
X	disastrous (buildings destroyed, rails bend)
XI	very disastrous (landslides, few buildings survive)
XII	catastrophic (total destruction)

Listed below are the Mercalli and Richter scales, with equivalents in joules, and a table comparing the Richter scale with joules.

Mercalli	Richter	Joules	Richter	Joules
I	<3.5	$<1.6 \times 10^7$ J	0	6.3×10^{-2} J
II	3.5	1.6×10^7 J	1	1.6×10 J
III	4.2	7.5×10^8 J	2	4.0×10^3 J
IV	4.5	4.0×10^9 J	3	1.0×10^6 J
V	4.8	2.1×10^{10} J	4	2.5×10^8 J
VI	5.4	5.7×10^{11} J	5	6.3×10^{10} J
VII	6.1	2.8×10^{13} J	6	1.6×10^{13} J
VIII	6.5	2.5×10^{14} J	7	4.0×10^{15} J
IX	6.9	2.3×10^{15} J	8	1.0×10^{18} J
X	7.3	2.1×10^{16} J	9	2.5×10^{20} J
XI	8.1	1.7×10^{18} J	10	6.3×10^{22} J
XII	>8.1	$>1.7 \times 10^{18}$ J		

Actual earthquakes

The table below lists the year of selected earthquakes in different parts of the world and where they occurred, as well as the Richter magnitude of each.

Earthquakes	Richter
Assam, India (1897)	8.7
Alaska, USA (1964)	8.6
Concepción, Chile (1960)	8.5
San Francisco, USA (1906)	8.25
Mexico City, Mexico (1985)	8.1
Guatemala (1976)	7.9
Tangshan, China (1976)	7.6
Messina, Italy (1908)	7.5
Vrancea, Romania (1977)	7.2
San Francisco, USA (1989)	6.9

Decibels

The loudness of a sound is measured by the size of its vibrations; this is measured in decibels (dB).

Decibel scale

The dB scale is relative and increases exponentially, beginning with the smallest sound change that can be heard by humans (0–1 dB). A 20 dB sound is 10 times louder than a 10 dB sound; a 30 dB sound is 100 times as loud as that. Noises at the level of 120–130 dB can cause pain in humans; higher levels can cause permanent ear damage. The dB ratings (at certain distances) of some common noises are listed on page 135.

Wave amplitude

Amplitude is the distance between a wave peak or trough and an intermediate line of equilibrium (**a**). The greater the amount of energy transmitted in a sound wave, the greater is the wave's amplitude and the louder the sound heard.

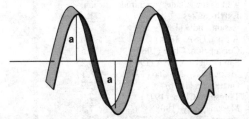

A	0 dB	human minimum audibility	
B	30 dB	soft whisper at 5 m	
C	50 dB	inside urban home	
D	55 dB	light traffic at 15 m	
E	60 dB	conversation at 1 m	
F	85 dB	pneumatic drill at 15 m	
G	90 dB	heavy traffic at 15 m	
H	100 dB	loud shout at 15 m	
I	105 dB	aeroplane take-off at 600 m	
J	117 dB	inside full-volume disco	
K	120 dB	aeroplane take-off at 60 m	
L	130 dB	pain threshold for humans	
M	140 dB	aeroplane take-off at 30 m	

Energy needs by activity

	Activity	☐ Women	■ Men
A	Sleeping	230 kJ; 55 kcal	272 kJ; 65 kcal
B	Sitting	293 kJ; 70 kcal	377 kJ; 90 kcal
C	Standing	419 kJ; 100 kcal	502 kJ; 120 kcal
D	Walking	754 kJ; 180 kcal	921 kJ; 220 kcal
E	Walking (uphill)	1507 kJ; 360 kcal	1842 kJ; 440 kcal
F	Running	1759 kJ; 420 kcal	2512 kJ; 600 kcal

Men use more kilocalories than women for all activities because men have more weight to carry around, and because women usually have more body fat and so need less energy to retain body heat.

Energy values of selected foods

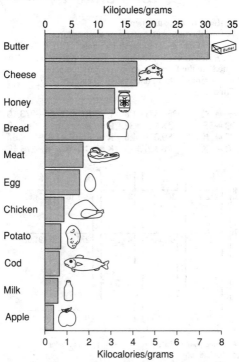

6: Temperature

Systems of measurement

Below, the different systems of temperature measurement are compared: Fahrenheit (°F), Celsius (°C), Réaumur (°r), Rankine (°R) and Kelvin (K). Also listed are the formulas for converting temperature measurements from one system to another.

Formulas

°F ➡ °C	(°F−32)÷1.8	°r ➡ K	(°r×1.25)+273.16
°C ➡ °F	(°C×1.8)+32	°R ➡ K	°R÷1.8
°F ➡ K	(°F+459.67)÷1.8	K ➡ °F	(K×1.8)−459.67
°C ➡ K	°C+273.16	K ➡ °C	K−273.16

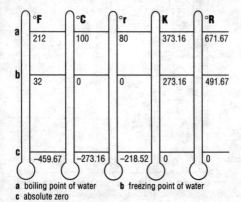

	°F	°C	°r	K	°R
a	212	100	80	373.16	671.67
b	32	0	0	273.16	491.67
c	−459.67	−273.16	−218.52	0	0

a boiling point of water **b** freezing point of water
c absolute zero

Conversion tables

The tables below list the equivalent units of temperature in the Fahrenheit, Celsius and Kelvin systems.

Fahrenheit to Celsius to Kelvin			Fahrenheit to Celsius to Kelvin		
°F	°C	K	°F	°C	K
−40.0	−40	233	−4.0	−20	253
−38.2	−39	234	−2.2	−19	254
−36.4	−38	235	−0.4	−18	255
−34.6	−37	236	1.4	−17	256
−32.8	−36	237	3.2	−16	257
−31.0	−35	238	5.0	−15	258
−29.2	−34	239	6.8	−14	259
−27.4	−33	240	8.6	−13	260
−25.6	−32	241	10.4	−12	261
−23.8	−31	242	12.2	−11	262
−22.0	−30	243	14.0	−10	263
−20.2	−29	244	15.8	−9	264
−18.4	−28	245	17.6	−8	265
−16.6	−27	246	19.4	−7	266
−14.8	−26	247	21.2	−6	267
−13.0	−25	248	23.0	−5	268
−11.2	−24	249	24.8	−4	269
−9.4	−23	250	26.6	−3	270
−7.6	−22	251	28.4	−2	271
−5.8	−21	252	30.2	−1	272

Fahrenheit, Celsius and Kelvin unit equivalents (continued)

Fahrenheit to Celsius to Kelvin				Fahrenheit to Celsius to Kelvin		
°F	°C	K		°F	°C	K
32.0	0	273		68.0	20	293
33.8	1	274		69.8	21	294
35.6	2	275		71.6	22	295
37.4	3	276		73.4	23	296
39.2	4	277		75.2	24	297
41.0	5	278		77.0	25	298
42.8	6	279		78.8	26	299
44.6	7	280		80.6	27	300
46.4	8	281		82.4	28	301
48.2	9	282		84.2	29	302
50.0	10	283		86.0	30	303
51.8	11	284		87.8	31	304
53.6	12	285		89.6	32	305
55.4	13	286		91.4	33	306
57.2	14	287		93.2	34	307
59.0	15	288		95.0	35	308
60.8	16	289		95.0	36	309
62.6	17	290		98.6	37	310
64.4	18	291		100.4	38	311
66.2	19	292		102.2	39	312

Fahrenheit to Celsius to Kelvin				Fahrenheit to Celsius to Kelvin		
°F	°C	K		°F	°C	K
104.0	40	313		140.0	60	333
105.8	41	314		141.8	61	334
107.6	42	315		143.6	62	335
109.4	43	316		145.4	63	336
111.2	44	317		147.2	64	337
113.0	45	318		149.0	65	338
114.8	46	319		150.8	66	339
116.6	47	320		152.6	67	340
116.6	48	321		154.4	68	341
120.2	49	322		156.2	69	342
122.0	50	323		158.0	70	343
123.8	51	324		159.8	71	344
125.6	55	325		161.6	72	345
127.4	53	326		163.4	73	346
129.2	54	327		165.2	74	347
131.0	55	328		167.0	75	348
132.8	56	329		168.8	76	349
134.6	57	330		170.6	77	350
136.4	58	331		172.4	78	351
136.4	59	332		174.2	79	352

Fahrenheit, Celsius and Kelvin unit equivalents (continued)

Fahrenheit to Celsius to Kelvin			Fahrenheit to Celsius to Kelvin		
°F	°C	K	°F	°C	K
176.0	80	353	212.0	100	373
177.8	81	354	213.8	101	374
179.6	82	355	215.6	102	375
181.4	83	356	217.4	103	376
183.2	84	357	219.2	104	377
185.0	85	358	221.0	105	378
186.8	86	359	222.8	106	379
188.6	87	360	224.6	107	380
190.4	88	361	226.4	108	381
192.2	89	362	228.2	109	382
194.0	90	363	230.0	110	383
195.8	91	364	231.8	111	384
197.6	92	365	233.6	112	385
199.4	93	366	235.4	113	386
201.2	94	367	237.2	114	387
203.0	95	368	239.0	115	388
204.8	96	369	240.8	116	389
206.6	97	370	242.6	117	390
208.4	98	371	244.4	118	391
210.2	99	372	246.2	119	392

Useful temperatures

Quick temperature reference

Condition	°C	°F
Water freezes	0	32
Mild winter day	10	50
Warm spring day	20	68
Hot summer day	30	86
Body temperature	37	98.6
Heat wave	40	104
Water boils	100	212

Oven temperatures

Below is a table of Fahrenheit/Celsius conversions for common oven temperatures.

°F	°C	Oven
225	110	very cool
250	130	
275	140	cool
300	150	
325	170	moderate
350	180	
375	190	moderately hot
400	200	
425	220	hot
450	230	
475	240	very hot

For other conversions, use the following formulas:

°F to °C Subtract 32, then divide by $9 \div 5$ (which equals 1.8).

°C to °F Multiply by $9 \div 5$ (which equals 1.8), then add 32.

7: Time

Units of time
Listed below are the ways of measuring time that are
artificially derived, as opposed to astronomical
methods.

Years, months, weeks
Below are some widely used names for periods of time.

Name	Period	Name	Period
millennium	1000	leap year	366 days
half-millennium	500	year	365 days
century	100	year	12 months
half-century	50	year	52 weeks
decade	10	month	28–31 days
half-decade	5	week	7 days

Days, hours, minutes
Below are listed the basic subdivisions of a day and
their equivalents.

1 day = 24 hours = 1440 minutes = 86 400 seconds
1 hour = $1/24$ day = 60 minutes = 3600 seconds
1 minute = $1/1440$ day = $1/60$ hour = 60 seconds
1 second = $1/86\,400$ day = $1/3600$ hour = $1/60$ minute

Seconds
Greater precision in measuring time has required
seconds (s) to be broken down into smaller units, using
standard metric prefixes.

1 terasecond (Ts)	10^{12} s	31 689 years
1 gigasecond (Gs)	10^9 s	31.7 years
1 megasecond (Ms)	10^6 s	11.6 days
1 kilosecond (ks)	10^3 s	16.67 minutes

1 millisecond (ms)	10^{-3} s	0.001 seconds
1 microsecond (μs)	10^{-6} s	0.000 001
1 nanosecond (ns)	10^{-9} s	0.000 000 001
1 picosecond (ps)	10^{-12} s	0.000 000 000 001
1 femtosecond (fs)	10^{-15} s	0.000 000 000 000 001
1 attosecond (as)	10^{-18} s	0.000 000 000 000 000 001

Astronomical time

Time can be measured by motion; in fact, the motion of the Earth, Sun, Moon and stars provided humans with the first means of measuring time.

Years, months, days

Sidereal times are calculated by the Earth's position according to fixed stars. The anomalistic year is measured according to the Earth's orbit in relation to the perihelion (Earth's minimum distance to the Sun). Tropical times refer to the apparent passage of the Sun and the actual passage of the Moon across Earth's equatorial plane. The synodic month is based on the phases of the Moon. Solar time (as in a mean solar day) refers to periods of darkness and light averaged over a year.

Time	Days	Hours	Minutes	Seconds
sidereal year	365	6	9	10
anomalistic year	365	6	13	53
tropical year	365	5	48	45
sidereal month	27	7	43	11
tropical month	27	7	43	5
synodic month	29	12	44	3
mean solar day	0	24	0	0
sidereal day	0	23	56	4

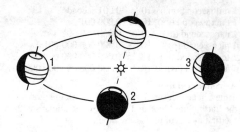

Equinox and solstice

The inclination of the Earth to its plane of rotation
around the Sun produces variations in the lengths of
day and night at different times of the year. Solstices
are when the Sun appears to be overhead at midday at
the maximum distances north and south of the Equator.
At the summer solstice, days are longest and nights are
shortest; this is reversed at the winter solstice.
Equinoxes are when day and night are equal every-
where; at these times, the Sun appears overhead at
midday at the Equator.

The table lists the dates of the solstices and equinox
in each hemisphere, keyed by number to the diagram
above, which shows the Earth at four points in its orbit.

Date	Northern	Southern
1 21 June	summer solstice	winter solstice
2 23 Sept.	autumn equinox	spring equinox
3 22 Dec.	winter solstice	summer solstice
4 21 March	spring equinox	autumn equinox

Years and seasons

Seasonal variations are another result of the inclination of the Earth's axis to its plane of rotation around the Sun. Parts of the globe tilted away from the Sun receive less radiant energy per unit area than those receiving rays more directly. The table below lists the seasonal equivalents in the two hemispheres, keyed by number to the diagram opposite.

Northern	**Southern**
1 summer	winter
2 autumn	spring
3 winter	summer
4 spring	autumn

Length of days

a Arctic Circle: 66° 33′N – 24 hours daylight
b 49° 3′N – 16 hours daylight
c The Equator: 0° – 12 hours daylight
d 49° 3′S – 8 hours daylight
e Antarctic Circle: 66° 33′S – 0 hours daylight

The diagram above illustrates the variety in the length of the day (21 June) at different latitudes (° = degrees; ′ = minute). On this day, the northern hemisphere receives the maximum hours of daylight; the southern hemisphere, the minimum.

Geological timescale

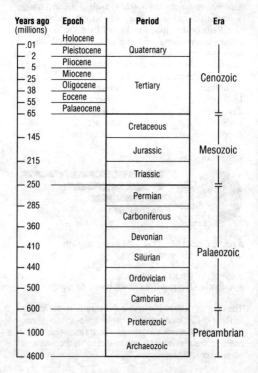

Years ago (millions)	Epoch	Period	Era
.01	Holocene	Quaternary	
2	Pleistocene	Quaternary	Cenozoic
5	Pliocene		
25	Miocene		
38	Oligocene	Tertiary	
55	Eocene		
65	Palaeocene		
145		Cretaceous	Mesozoic
215		Jurassic	
250		Triassic	
285		Permian	Palaeozoic
360		Carboniferous	
410		Devonian	
440		Silurian	
500		Ordovician	
600		Cambrian	
1000		Proterozoic	Precambrian
4600		Archaeozoic	

The zodiac year

Aries
Ram
*(March 21-
April 20)*

Taurus
Bull
*(April 21-
May 20)*

Gemini
Twins
*(May 21-
June 20)*

Cancer
Crab
*(June 21-
July 21)*

Leo
Lion
*(July 22-
August 21)*

Virgo
Virgin
*(August 22-
September 21)*

Libra
Scales
*(Sepember 22-
October 22)*

Scorpio
Scorpion
*(October 23-
November 21)*

Sagittarius
Archer
*(November 22-
December 20)*

Capricorn
Goat
*(December 21-
January 19)*

Aquarius
Water-bearer
*(January 20-
February 18)*

Pisces
Fish
*(February 19-
March 20)*

Types of calendar
The number of days in a year varies among cultures
and from year to year.

Gregorian
The Gregorian calendar is a 16th-century adaptation of
the Julian calendar devised in the 1st century BC. The
year in this calendar is based on the solar year, which
lasts about 365 $1/4$ days. In this system, years whose
number is not divisible by 4 have 365 days, as do
centennial years unless the figures before the noughts
are divisible by 4. All other years have 366 days; these
are leap years.

Below are the names of the months and number of
days for a non-leap year.

January	31	July	31
February	28*	August	31
March	31	September	30
April	30	October	31
May	31	November	30
June	30	December	31

* 29 in leap years.

Jewish
A year in the Jewish calendar has 13 months if its
number, when divided by 9, leaves 0, 3, 6, 8, 11, 14 or
17; otherwise, it has 12 months. The year is based on the
lunar year, but its number of months varies to keep
broadly in line with the solar cycle. Its precise number
of days is fixed with reference to particular festivals
that must not fall on certain days of the week.

Below are the names of the months and number of days in each for the year 5471, a 12-month year (1980 AD in Gregorian).

Tishri	30	Nisan	30
Cheshvan	29*	Iyar	29
Kislev	29*	Sivan	30
Tevet	29	Tammuz	29
Shevat	30	Av	30
Adar	29†	Elul	29

* 30 in some years.
† In 13-month years, the month Veadar, with 29 days, falls between Adar and Nisan.

Muslim

A year in the Muslim calendar has 355 days if its number, when divided by 30, leaves 2, 5, 7, 10, 13, 16, 18, 21, 24, 26 or 29; otherwise it has 354 days. As in the Jewish calendar, years are based on the lunar cycle.

Below are the names of the months and number of days in each for the Muslim year 1401 (1980 AD in Gregorian).

Muharram	30	Rajab	30
Safar	29	Sha'ban	29
Rabi'I	30	Ramadan	30
Rabi'II	29	Shawwal	29
Jumada I	30	Dhu l-Qa'dah	30
Jumada II	29	Dhu l-Hijja	30*

* 29 in some years.

Wedding anniversaries

Year	Traditional (alternative)	Modern
1st	Paper	Clocks
2nd	Cotton	China
3rd	Leather	Crystal, glass
4th	Linen (silk)	Electrical appliances
5th	Wood	Silverware
6th	Iron	Wood
7th	Wool (copper)	Desk sets
8th	Bronze	Linens, lace
9th	Pottery (china)	Leather
10th	Tin (aluminium)	Diamond jewellery
11th	Steel	Fashion jewellery, accessories
12th	Silk	Pearls or coloured gems
13th	Lace	Textile, furs
14th	Ivory	Gold jewellery
15th	Crystal	Watches
20th	China	Platinum
25th	Silver	Sterling silver jubilee
30th	Pearl	Diamond
35th	Coral (jade)	Jade
40th	Ruby	Ruby
45th	Sapphire	Sapphire
50th	Gold	Gold
55th	Emerald	Emerald
60th	Diamond	Diamond

Perpetual calendar
How to use the calendar To discover on which day of the week any date between the years 1780 and 2014 falls, look up the year in the key and the letter shown to the right will indicate which of the calendars A–N you should consult.

Key:

Year		Year		Year	
1780	N	1805	C	1830	F
1781	B	1806	D	1831	G
1782	C	1807	E	1832	H
1783	D	1808	M	1833	C
1784	L	1809	A	1834	D
1785	G	1810	B	1835	E
1786	A	1811	C	1836	M
1787	B	1812	K	1837	A
1788	J	1813	F	1838	B
1789	E	1814	G	1839	C
1790	F	1815	A	1840	K
1791	G	1816	I	1841	F
1792	H	1817	D	1842	G
1793	C	1818	E	1843	A
1794	D	1819	F	1844	I
1795	E	1820	N	1845	D
1796	M	1821	B	1846	E
1797	A	1822	C	1847	F
1798	B	1823	D	1848	N
1799	C	1824	L	1849	B
1800	D	1825	G	1850	C
1801	E	1826	A	1851	D
1802	F	1827	B	1852	L
1803	G	1828	J	1853	G
1804	H	1829	E	1854	A

Year	Code	Year	Code	Year	Code
1855	B	1887	G	1919	D
1856	J	1888	H	1920	L
1857	E	1889	C	1921	G
1858	F	1890	D	1922	A
1859	G	1891	E	1923	B
1860	H	1892	M	1924	J
1861	C	1893	A	1925	E
1862	D	1894	B	1926	F
1863	E	1895	C	1927	G
1864	M	1896	K	1928	H
1865	A	1897	F	1929	C
1866	B	1898	G	1930	D
1867	C	1899	A	1931	E
1868	K	1900	B	1932	M
1869	F	1901	C	1933	A
1870	G	1902	D	1934	B
1871	A	1903	E	1935	C
1872	I	1904	M	1936	K
1873	D	1905	A	1937	F
1874	E	1906	B	1938	G
1875	F	1907	C	1939	A
1876	N	1908	K	1940	I
1877	B	1909	F	1941	D
1878	C	1910	G	1942	E
1879	D	1911	A	1943	F
1880	L	1912	I	1944	N
1881	G	1913	D	1945	B
1882	A	1914	E	1946	C
1883	B	1915	F	1947	D
1884	J	1916	N	1948	L
1885	E	1917	B	1949	G
1886	F	1918	C	1950	A

Year	Code	Year	Code
1951	B	1983	G
1952	J	1984	H
1953	E	1985	C
1954	F	1986	D
1955	G	1987	E
1956	H	1988	M
1957	C	1989	A
1958	D	1990	B
1959	E	1991	C
1960	M	1992	K
1961	A	1993	F
1962	B	1994	G
1963	C	1995	A
1964	K	1996	I
1965	F	1997	D
1966	G	1998	E
1967	A	1999	F
1968	I	2000	N
1969	D	2001	B
1970	E	2002	C
1971	F	2003	D
1972	N	2004	L
1973	B	2005	G
1974	C	2006	A
1975	D	2007	B
1976	L	2008	J
1977	G	2009	E
1978	A	2010	F
1979	B	2011	G
1980	J	2012	H
1981	E	2013	C
1982	F	2014	D

A   1786 1797 1809 1815 1826 1837 1843
1854 1865 1871 1882 1893 1899 1905

JANUARY

S	M	T	W	T	F	S
1	2	3	4	5	6	7
8	9	10	11	12	13	14
15	16	17	18	19	20	21
22	23	24	25	26	27	28
29	30	31				

FEBRUARY

S	M	T	W	T	F	S
			1	2	3	4
5	6	7	8	9	10	11
12	13	14	15	16	17	18
19	20	21	22	23	24	25
26	27	28				

MARCH

S	M	T	W	T	F	S
			1	2	3	4
5	6	7	8	9	10	11
12	13	14	15	16	17	18
19	20	21	22	23	24	25
26	27	28	29	30	31	

APRIL

S	M	T	W	T	F	S
						1
2	3	4	5	6	7	8
9	10	11	12	13	14	15
16	17	18	19	20	21	22
23	24	25	26	27	28	29
30						

MAY

S	M	T	W	T	F	S
	1	2	3	4	5	6
7	8	9	10	11	12	13
14	15	16	17	18	19	20
21	22	23	24	25	26	27
28	29	30	31			

JUNE

S	M	T	W	T	F	S
				1	2	3
4	5	6	7	8	9	10
11	12	13	14	15	16	17
18	19	20	21	22	23	24
25	26	27	28	29	30	

1911 1922 1933 1939 1950 1961 1967 1978 1989 1995 2006 **A**

JULY

S	M	T	W	T	F	S
						1
2	3	4	5	6	7	8
9	10	11	12	13	14	15
16	17	18	19	20	21	22
23	24	25	26	27	28	29
30	31					

AUGUST

S	M	T	W	T	F	S
		1	2	3	4	5
6	7	8	9	10	11	12
13	14	15	16	17	18	19
20	21	22	23	24	25	26
27	28	29	30	31		

SEPTEMBER

S	M	T	W	T	F	S
					1	2
3	4	5	6	7	8	9
10	11	12	13	14	15	16
17	18	19	20	21	22	23
24	25	26	27	28	29	30

OCTOBER

S	M	T	W	T	F	S
1	2	3	4	5	6	7
8	9	10	11	12	13	14
15	16	17	18	19	20	21
22	23	24	25	26	27	28
29	30	31				

NOVEMBER

S	M	T	W	T	F	S
			1	2	3	4
5	6	7	8	9	10	11
12	13	14	15	16	17	18
19	20	21	22	23	24	25
26	27	28	29	30		

DECEMBER

S	M	T	W	T	F	S
					1	2
3	4	5	6	7	8	9
10	11	12	13	14	15	16
17	18	19	20	21	22	23
24	25	26	27	28	29	30
31						

B   1781   1787   1798   1810   1821   1827   1838
       1849   1855   1866   1877   1883   1894   1900

JANUARY

S	M	T	W	T	F	S
	1	2	3	4	5	6
7	8	9	10	11	12	13
14	15	16	17	18	19	20
21	22	23	24	25	26	27
28	29	30	31			

FEBRUARY

S	M	T	W	T	F	S
				1	2	3
4	5	6	7	8	9	10
11	12	13	14	15	16	17
18	19	20	21	22	23	24
25	26	27	28			

MARCH

S	M	T	W	T	F	S
				1	2	3
4	5	6	7	8	9	10
11	12	13	14	15	16	17
18	19	20	21	22	23	24
25	26	27	28	29	30	31

APRIL

S	M	T	W	T	F	S
1	2	3	4	5	6	7
8	9	10	11	12	13	14
15	16	17	18	19	20	21
22	23	24	25	26	27	28
29	30					

MAY

S	M	T	W	T	F	S
		1	2	3	4	5
6	7	8	9	10	11	12
13	14	15	16	17	18	19
20	21	22	23	24	25	26
27	28	29	30	31		

JUNE

S	M	T	W	T	F	S
					1	2
3	4	5	6	7	8	9
10	11	12	13	14	15	16
17	18	19	20	21	22	23
24	25	26	27	28	29	30

1906 1917 1923 1934 1945 1951 1962
1973 1979 1990 2001 2007 **B**

JULY

S	M	T	W	T	F	S
	1	2	3	4	5	6	7
8	9	10	11	12	13	14
15	16	17	18	19	20	21
22	23	24	25	26	27	28
29	30	31				

AUGUST

S	M	T	W	T	F	S
			1	2	3	4
5	6	7	8	9	10	11
12	13	14	15	16	17	18
19	20	21	22	23	24	25
26	27	28	29	30	31	

SEPTEMBER

S	M	T	W	T	F	S
						1
2	3	4	5	6	7	8
9	10	11	12	13	14	15
16	17	18	19	20	21	22
23	24	25	26	27	28	29
30						

OCTOBER

S	M	T	W	T	F	S
	1	2	3	4	5	6
7	8	9	10	11	12	13
14	15	16	17	18	19	20
21	22	23	24	25	26	27
28	29	30	31			

NOVEMBER

S	M	T	W	T	F	S
				1	2	3
4	5	6	7	8	9	10
11	12	13	14	15	16	17
18	19	20	21	22	23	24
25	26	27	28	29	30	

DECEMBER

S	M	T	W	T	F	S
						1
2	3	4	5	6	7	8
9	10	11	12	13	14	15
16	17	18	19	20	21	22
23	24	25	26	27	28	29
30	31					

C

| 1782 | 1793 | 1799 | 1805 | 1811 | 1822 | 1833 |
| 1839 | 1850 | 1861 | 1867 | 1878 | 1889 | 1895 |

JANUARY

S	M	T	W	T	F	S
			1	2	3	4	5
6	7	8	9	10	11	12
13	14	15	16	17	18	19
20	21	22	23	24	25	26
27	28	29	30	31		

FEBRUARY

S	M	T	W	T	F	S
					1	2
3	4	5	6	7	8	9
10	11	12	13	14	15	16
17	18	19	20	21	22	23
24	25	26	27	28		

MARCH

S	M	T	W	T	F	S
					1	2
3	4	5	6	7	8	9
10	11	12	13	14	15	16
17	18	19	20	21	22	23
24	25	26	27	28	29	30
31						

APRIL

S	M	T	W	T	F	S
	1	2	3	4	5	6
7	8	9	10	11	12	13
14	15	16	17	18	19	20
21	22	23	24	25	26	27
28	29	30				

MAY

S	M	T	W	T	F	S
			1	2	3	4
5	6	7	8	9	10	11
12	13	14	15	16	17	18
19	20	21	22	23	24	25
26	27	28	29	30	31	

JUNE

S	M	T	W	T	F	S
						1
2	3	4	5	6	7	8
9	10	11	12	13	14	15
16	17	18	19	20	21	22
23	24	25	26	27	28	29
30						

**1901 1907 1918 1929 1935 1946 1957
1963 1974 1985 1991 2002 2013** **C**

JULY

S	M	T	W	T	F	S
	1	2	3	4	5	6
7	8	9	10	11	12	13
14	15	16	17	18	19	20
21	22	23	24	25	26	27
28	29	30	31			

AUGUST

S	M	T	W	T	F	S
				1	2	3
4	5	6	7	8	9	10
11	12	13	14	15	16	17
18	19	20	21	22	23	24
25	26	27	28	29	30	31

SEPTEMBER

S	M	T	W	T	F	S
1	2	3	4	5	6	7
8	9	10	11	12	13	14
15	16	17	18	19	20	21
22	23	24	25	26	27	28
29	30					

OCTOBER

S	M	T	W	T	F	S
		1	2	3	4	5
6	7	8	9	10	11	12
13	14	15	16	17	18	19
20	21	22	23	24	25	26
27	28	29	30	31		

NOVEMBER

S	M	T	W	T	F	S
					1	2
3	4	5	6	7	8	9
10	11	12	13	14	15	16
17	18	19	20	21	22	23
24	25	26	27	28	29	30

DECEMBER

S	M	T	W	T	F	S
1	2	3	4	5	6	7
8	9	10	11	12	13	14
15	16	17	18	19	20	21
22	23	24	25	26	27	28
29	30	31				

D
1783 1794 1800 1806 1817 1823 1834
1845 1851 1862 1873 1879 1890 1902

JANUARY

S	M	T	W	T	F	S
			1	2	3	4
5	6	7	8	9	10	11
12	13	14	15	16	17	18
19	20	21	22	23	24	25
26	27	28	29	30	31	

FEBRUARY

S	M	T	W	T	F	S
						1
2	3	4	5	6	7	8
9	10	11	12	13	14	15
16	17	18	19	20	21	22
23	24	25	26	27	28	

MARCH

S	M	T	W	T	F	S
						1
2	3	4	5	6	7	8
9	10	11	12	13	14	15
16	17	18	19	20	21	22
23	24	25	26	27	28	29
30	31					

APRIL

S	M	T	W	T	F	S
		1	2	3	4	5
6	7	8	9	10	11	12
13	14	15	16	17	18	19
20	21	22	23	24	25	26
27	28	29	30			

MAY

S	M	T	W	T	F	S
				1	2	3
4	5	6	7	8	9	10
11	12	13	14	15	16	17
18	19	20	21	22	23	24
25	26	27	28	29	30	31

JUNE

S	M	T	W	T	F	S
1	2	3	4	5	6	7
8	9	10	11	12	13	14
15	16	17	18	19	20	21
22	23	24	25	26	27	28
29	30					

1913 1919 1930 1941 1947 1958 1969 1975 1986 1997 2003 2014 **D**

JULY

S	M	T	W	T	F	S
		1	2	3	4	5
6	7	8	9	10	11	12
13	14	15	16	17	18	19
20	21	22	23	24	25	26
27	28	29	30	31		

AUGUST

S	M	T	W	T	F	S
					1	2
3	4	5	6	7	8	9
10	11	12	13	14	15	16
17	18	19	20	21	22	23
24	25	26	27	28	29	30
31						

SEPTEMBER

S	M	T	W	T	F	S
	1	2	3	4	5	6
7	8	9	10	11	12	13
14	15	16	17	18	19	20
21	22	23	24	25	26	27
28	29	30				

OCTOBER

S	M	T	W	T	F	S
			1	2	3	4
5	6	7	8	9	10	11
12	13	14	15	16	17	18
19	20	21	22	23	24	25
26	27	28	29	30	31	

NOVEMBER

S	M	T	W	T	F	S
						1
2	3	4	5	6	7	8
9	10	11	12	13	14	15
16	17	18	19	20	21	22
23	24	25	26	27	28	29
30						

DECEMBER

S	M	T	W	T	F	S
	1	2	3	4	5	6
7	8	9	10	11	12	13
14	15	16	17	18	19	20
21	22	23	24	25	26	27
28	29	30	31			

E 1789 1795 1801 1807 1818 1829 1835
       1846 1857 1863 1874 1885 1891 1903

JANUARY

S	M	T	W	T	F	S
				1	2	3
4	5	6	7	8	9	10
11	12	13	14	15	16	17
18	19	20	21	22	23	24
25	26	27	28	29	30	31

FEBRUARY

S	M	T	W	T	F	S
1	2	3	4	5	6	7
8	9	10	11	12	13	14
15	16	17	18	19	20	21
22	23	24	25	26	27	28

MARCH

S	M	T	W	T	F	S
1	2	3	4	5	6	7
8	9	10	11	12	13	14
15	16	17	18	19	20	21
22	23	24	25	26	27	28
29	30	31				

APRIL

S	M	T	W	T	F	S
			1	2	3	4
5	6	7	8	9	10	11
12	13	14	15	16	17	18
19	20	21	22	23	24	25
26	27	28	29	30		

MAY

S	M	T	W	T	F	S
					1	2
3	4	5	6	7	8	9
10	11	12	13	14	15	16
17	18	19	20	21	22	23
24	25	26	27	28	29	30
31						

JUNE

S	M	T	W	T	F	S
	1	2	3	4	5	6
7	8	9	10	11	12	13
14	15	16	17	18	19	20
21	22	23	24	25	26	27
28	29	30				

1914 1925 1931 1942 1953 1959 1970 1981 1987 1998 2009

E

JULY
S	M	T	W	T	F	S
		1	2	3	4	
5	6	7	8	9	10	11
12	13	14	15	16	17	18
19	20	21	22	23	24	25
26	27	28	29	30	31	

AUGUST
S	M	T	W	T	F	S
						1
2	3	4	5	6	7	8
9	10	11	12	13	14	15
16	17	18	19	20	21	22
23	24	25	26	27	28	29
30	31					

SEPTEMBER
S	M	T	W	T	F	S
		1	2	3	4	5
6	7	8	9	10	11	12
13	14	15	16	17	18	19
20	21	22	23	24	25	26
27	28	29	30			

OCTOBER
S	M	T	W	T	F	S
				1	2	3
4	5	6	7	8	9	10
11	12	13	14	15	16	17
18	19	20	21	22	23	24
25	26	27	28	29	30	31

NOVEMBER
S	M	T	W	T	F	S
1	2	3	4	5	6	7
8	9	10	11	12	13	14
15	16	17	18	19	20	21
22	23	24	25	26	27	28
29	30					

DECEMBER
S	M	T	W	T	F	S
		1	2	3	4	5
6	7	8	9	10	11	12
13	14	15	16	17	18	19
20	21	22	23	24	25	26
27	28	29	30	31		

F 1790 1802 1813 1819 1830 1841 1847
1858 1869 1875 1886 1897 1909 1915

JANUARY

S	M	T	W	T	F	S
					1	2
3	4	5	6	7	8	9
10	11	12	13	14	15	16
17	18	19	20	21	22	23
24	25	26	27	28	29	30
31						

FEBRUARY

S	M	T	W	T	F	S
	1	2	3	4	5	6
7	8	9	10	11	12	13
14	15	16	17	18	19	20
21	22	23	24	25	26	27
28						

MARCH

S	M	T	W	T	F	S
	1	2	3	4	5	6
7	8	9	10	11	12	13
14	15	16	17	18	19	20
21	22	23	24	25	26	27
28	29	30	31			

APRIL

S	M	T	W	T	F	S
				1	2	3
4	5	6	7	8	9	10
11	12	13	14	15	16	17
18	19	20	21	22	23	24
25	26	27	28	29	30	

MAY

S	M	T	W	T	F	S
						1
2	3	4	5	6	7	8
9	10	11	12	13	14	15
16	17	18	19	20	21	22
23	24	25	26	27	28	29
30	31					

JUNE

S	M	T	W	T	F	S
		1	2	3	4	5
6	7	8	9	10	11	12
13	14	15	16	17	18	19
20	21	22	23	24	25	26
27	28	29	30			

1926 1937 1943 1954 1965 1971 1982 1993 1999 2010 **F**

JULY

S	M	T	W	T	F	S
				1	2	3
4	5	6	7	8	9	10
11	12	13	14	15	16	17
18	19	20	21	22	23	24
25	26	27	28	29	30	31

AUGUST

S	M	T	W	T	F	S
1	2	3	4	5	6	7
8	9	10	11	12	13	14
15	16	17	18	19	20	21
22	23	24	25	26	27	28
29	30	31				

SEPTEMBER

S	M	T	W	T	F	S
			1	2	3	4
5	6	7	8	9	10	11
12	13	14	15	16	17	18
19	20	21	22	23	24	25
26	27	28	29	30		

OCTOBER

S	M	T	W	T	F	S
					1	2
3	4	5	6	7	8	9
10	11	12	13	14	15	16
17	18	19	20	21	22	23
24	25	26	27	28	29	30
31						

NOVEMBER

S	M	T	W	T	F	S
	1	2	3	4	5	6
7	8	9	10	11	12	13
14	15	16	17	18	19	20
21	22	23	24	25	26	27
28	29	30				

DECEMBER

S	M	T	W	T	F	S
			1	2	3	4
5	6	7	8	9	10	11
12	13	14	15	16	17	18
19	20	21	22	23	24	25
26	27	28	29	30	31	

G 1785 1791 1803 1814 1825 1831 1842
       1853 1859 1870 1881 1887 1898 1910

JANUARY

S	M	T	W	T	F	S
						1
2	3	4	5	6	7	8
9	10	11	12	13	14	15
16	17	18	19	20	21	22
23	24	25	26	27	28	29
30	31					

FEBRUARY

S	M	T	W	T	F	S
		1	2	3	4	5
6	7	8	9	10	11	12
13	14	15	16	17	18	19
20	21	22	23	24	25	26
27	28					

MARCH

S	M	T	W	T	F	S
		1	2	3	4	5
6	7	8	9	10	11	12
13	14	15	16	17	18	19
20	21	22	23	24	25	26
27	28	29	30	31		

APRIL

S	M	T	W	T	F	S
					1	2
3	4	5	6	7	8	9
10	11	12	13	14	15	16
17	18	19	20	21	22	23
24	25	26	27	28	29	30

MAY

S	M	T	W	T	F	S
1	2	3	4	5	6	7
8	9	10	11	12	13	14
15	16	17	18	19	20	21
22	23	24	25	26	27	28
29	30	31				

JUNE

S	M	T	W	T	F	S
			1	2	3	4
5	6	7	8	9	10	11
12	13	14	15	16	17	18
19	20	21	22	23	24	25
26	27	28	29	30		

1921 1927 1938 1949 1955 1966 1977 **G**
1983 1994 2005 2011

JULY

S	M	T	W	T	F	S
					1	2
3	4	5	6	7	8	9
10	11	12	13	14	15	16
17	18	19	20	21	22	23
24	25	26	27	28	29	30
31						

AUGUST

S	M	T	W	T	F	S
	1	2	3	4	5	6
7	8	9	10	11	12	13
14	15	16	17	18	19	20
21	22	23	24	25	26	27
28	29	30	31			

SEPTEMBER

S	M	T	W	T	F	S
				1	2	3
4	5	6	7	8	9	10
11	12	13	14	15	16	17
18	19	20	21	22	23	24
25	26	27	28	29	30	

OCTOBER

S	M	T	W	T	F	S
						1
2	3	4	5	6	7	8
9	10	11	12	13	14	15
16	17	18	19	20	21	22
23	24	25	26	27	28	29
30	31					

NOVEMBER

S	M	T	W	T	F	S
		1	2	3	4	5
6	7	8	9	10	11	12
13	14	15	16	17	18	19
20	21	22	23	24	25	26
27	28	29	30			

DECEMBER

S	M	T	W	T	F	S
				1	2	3
4	5	6	7	8	9	10
11	12	13	14	15	16	17
18	19	20	21	22	23	24
25	26	27	28	29	30	31

H 1792 1804 1832 1860 1888
      1928 1956 1984 2012

JANUARY
S	M	T	W	T	F	S
	1	2	3	4	5	6	7
8	9	10	11	12	13	14
15	16	17	18	19	20	21
22	23	24	25	26	27	28
29	30	31				

FEBRUARY
S	M	T	W	T	F	S
			1	2	3	4
5	6	7	8	9	10	11
12	13	14	15	16	17	18
19	20	21	22	23	24	25
26	27	28	29			

MARCH
S	M	T	W	T	F	S
				1	2	3
4	5	6	7	8	9	10
11	12	13	14	15	16	17
18	19	20	21	22	23	24
25	26	27	28	29	30	31

APRIL
S	M	T	W	T	F	S
1	2	3	4	5	6	7
8	9	10	11	12	13	14
15	16	17	18	19	20	21
22	23	24	25	26	27	28
29	30					

MAY
S	M	T	W	T	F	S
		1	2	3	4	5
6	7	8	9	10	11	12
13	14	15	16	17	18	19
20	21	22	23	24	25	26
27	28	29	30	31		

JUNE
S	M	T	W	T	F	S
					1	2
3	4	5	6	7	8	9
10	11	12	13	14	15	16
17	18	19	20	21	22	23
24	25	26	27	28	29	30

H

JULY
S	M	T	W	T	F	S
1	2	3	4	5	6	7
8	9	10	11	12	13	14
15	16	17	18	19	20	21
22	23	24	25	26	27	28
29	30	31				

AUGUST
S	M	T	W	T	F	S
				1	2	3	4
5	6	7	8	9	10	11
12	13	14	15	16	17	18
19	20	21	22	23	24	25
26	27	28	29	30	31	

SEPTEMBER
S	M	T	W	T	F	S
						1
2	3	4	5	6	7	8
9	10	11	12	13	14	15
16	17	18	19	20	21	22
23	24	25	26	27	28	29
30						

OCTOBER
S	M	T	W	T	F	S
	1	2	3	4	5	6
7	8	9	10	11	12	13
14	15	16	17	18	19	20
21	22	23	24	25	26	27
28	29	30	31			

NOVEMBER
S	M	T	W	T	F	S
				1	2	3
4	5	6	7	8	9	10
11	12	13	14	15	16	17
18	19	20	21	22	23	24
25	26	27	28	29	30	

DECEMBER
S	M	T	W	T	F	S
						1
2	3	4	5	6	7	8
9	10	11	12	13	14	15
16	17	18	19	20	21	22
23	24	25	26	27	28	29
30	31					

I 1816 1844 1872 1912
       1940 1968 1996

JANUARY
S	M	T	W	T	F	S
		1	2	3	4	5	6
7	8	9	10	11	12	13
14	15	16	17	18	19	20
21	22	23	24	25	26	27
28	29	30	31			

FEBRUARY
S	M	T	W	T	F	S
					1	2	3
4	5	6	7	8	9	10
11	12	13	14	15	16	17
18	19	20	21	22	23	24
25	26	27	28	29		

MARCH
S	M	T	W	T	F	S
					1	2
3	4	5	6	7	8	9
10	11	12	13	14	15	16
17	18	19	20	21	22	23
24	25	26	27	28	29	30
31						

APRIL
S	M	T	W	T	F	S
	1	2	3	4	5	6
7	8	9	10	11	12	13
14	15	16	17	18	19	20
21	22	23	24	25	26	27
28	29	30				

MAY
S	M	T	W	T	F	S
			1	2	3	4
5	6	7	8	9	10	11
12	13	14	15	16	17	18
19	20	21	22	23	24	25
26	27	28	29	30	31	

JUNE
S	M	T	W	T	F	S
						1
2	3	4	5	6	7	8
9	10	11	12	13	14	15
16	17	18	19	20	21	22
23	24	25	26	27	28	29
30						

I

JULY

S	M	T	W	T	F	S
		1	2	3	4	5	6
7	8	9	10	11	12	13
14	15	16	17	18	19	20
21	22	23	24	25	26	27
28	29	30	31			

AUGUST

S	M	T	W	T	F	S
				1	2	3
4	5	6	7	8	9	10
11	12	13	14	15	16	17
18	19	20	21	22	23	24
25	26	27	28	29	30	31

SEPTEMBER

S	M	T	W	T	F	S
1	2	3	4	5	6	7
8	9	10	11	12	13	14
15	16	17	18	19	20	21
22	23	24	25	26	27	28
29	30					

OCTOBER

S	M	T	W	T	F	S
		1	2	3	4	5
6	7	8	9	10	11	12
13	14	15	16	17	18	19
20	21	22	23	24	25	26
27	28	29	30	31		

NOVEMBER

S	M	T	W	T	F	S
					1	2
3	4	5	6	7	8	9
10	11	12	13	14	15	16
17	18	19	20	21	22	23
24	25	26	27	28	29	30

DECEMBER

S	M	T	W	T	F	S
1	2	3	4	5	6	7
8	9	10	11	12	13	14
15	16	17	18	19	20	21
22	23	24	25	26	27	28
29	30	31				

J 1788 1828 1856 1884
       1924 1952 1980 2008

JANUARY
S	M	T	W	T	F	S
		1	2	3	4	5
6	7	8	9	10	11	12
13	14	15	16	17	18	19
20	21	22	23	24	25	26
27	28	29	30	31		

FEBRUARY
S	M	T	W	T	F	S
					1	2
3	4	5	6	7	8	9
10	11	12	13	14	15	16
17	18	19	20	21	22	23
24	25	26	27	28	29	

MARCH
S	M	T	W	T	F	S
						1
2	3	4	5	6	7	8
9	10	11	12	13	14	15
16	17	18	19	20	21	22
23	24	25	26	27	28	29
30	31					

APRIL
S	M	T	W	T	F	S
		1	2	3	4	5
6	7	8	9	10	11	12
13	14	15	16	17	18	19
20	21	22	23	24	25	26
27	28	29	30			

MAY
S	M	T	W	T	F	S
				1	2	3
4	5	6	7	8	9	10
11	12	13	14	15	16	17
18	19	20	21	22	23	24
25	26	27	28	29	30	31

JUNE
S	M	T	W	T	F	S
1	2	3	4	5	6	7
8	9	10	11	12	13	14
15	16	17	18	19	20	21
22	23	24	25	26	27	28
29	30					

J

JULY

S	M	T	W	T	F	S
		1	2	3	4	5
6	7	8	9	10	11	12
13	14	15	16	17	18	19
20	21	22	23	24	25	26
27	28	29	30	31		

AUGUST

S	M	T	W	T	F	S
					1	2
3	4	5	6	7	8	9
10	11	12	13	14	15	16
17	18	19	20	21	22	23
24	25	26	27	28	29	30
31						

SEPTEMBER

S	M	T	W	T	F	S
	1	2	3	4	5	6
7	8	9	10	11	12	13
14	15	16	17	18	19	20
21	22	23	24	25	26	27
28	29	30				

OCTOBER

S	M	T	W	T	F	S
			1	2	3	4
5	6	7	8	9	10	11
12	13	14	15	16	17	18
19	20	21	22	23	24	25
26	27	28	29	30	31	

NOVEMBER

S	M	T	W	T	F	S
						1
2	3	4	5	6	7	8
9	10	11	12	13	14	15
16	17	18	19	20	21	22
23	24	25	26	27	28	29
30						

DECEMBER

S	M	T	W	T	F	S
	1	2	3	4	5	6
7	8	9	10	11	12	13
14	15	16	17	18	19	20
21	22	23	24	25	26	27
28	29	30	31			

K 1812 1840 1868 1896
1908 1936 1864 1992

JANUARY
S	M	T	W	T	F	S
			1	2	3	4
5	6	7	8	9	10	11
12	13	14	15	16	17	18
19	20	21	22	23	24	25
26	27	28	29	30	31	

FEBRUARY
S	M	T	W	T	F	S
						1
2	3	4	5	6	7	8
9	10	11	12	13	14	15
16	17	18	19	20	21	22
23	24	25	26	27	28	29

MARCH
S	M	T	W	T	F	S
1	2	3	4	5	6	7
8	9	10	11	12	13	14
15	16	17	18	19	20	21
22	23	24	25	26	27	28
29	30	31				

APRIL
S	M	T	W	T	F	S
			1	2	3	4
5	6	7	8	9	10	11
12	13	14	15	16	17	18
19	20	21	22	23	24	25
26	27	28	29	30		

MAY
S	M	T	W	T	F	S
					1	2
3	4	5	6	7	8	9
10	11	12	13	14	15	16
17	18	19	20	21	22	23
24	25	26	27	28	29	30
31						

JUNE
S	M	T	W	T	F	S
	1	2	3	4	5	6
7	8	9	10	11	12	13
14	15	16	17	18	19	20
21	22	23	24	25	26	27
28	29	30				

K

JULY

S	M	T	W	T	F	S
			1	2	3	4
5	6	7	8	9	10	11
12	13	14	15	16	17	18
19	20	21	22	23	24	25
26	27	28	29	30	31	

AUGUST

S	M	T	W	T	F	S
						1
2	3	4	5	6	7	8
9	10	11	12	13	14	15
16	17	18	19	20	21	22
23	24	25	26	27	28	29
30	31					

SEPTEMBER

S	M	T	W	T	F	S
		1	2	3	4	5
6	7	8	9	10	11	12
13	14	15	16	17	18	19
20	21	22	23	24	25	26
27	28	29	30			

OCTOBER

S	M	T	W	T	F	S
				1	2	3
4	5	6	7	8	9	10
11	12	13	14	15	16	17
18	19	20	21	22	23	24
25	26	27	28	29	30	31

NOVEMBER

S	M	T	W	T	F	S
1	2	3	4	5	6	7
8	9	10	11	12	13	14
15	16	17	18	19	20	21
22	23	24	25	26	27	28
29	30					

DECEMBER

S	M	T	W	T	F	S
		1	2	3	4	5
6	7	8	9	10	11	12
13	14	15	16	17	18	19
20	21	22	23	24	25	26
27	28	29	30	31		

L   1784 1824 1852 1880
       1920 1948 1976 2004

JANUARY
S	M	T	W	T	F	S
				1	2	3
4	5	6	7	8	9	10
11	12	13	14	15	16	17
18	19	20	21	22	23	24
25	26	27	28	29	30	31

FEBRUARY
S	M	T	W	T	F	S
1	2	3	4	5	6	7
8	9	10	11	12	13	14
15	16	17	18	19	20	21
22	23	24	25	26	27	28
29						

MARCH
S	M	T	W	T	F	S
	1	2	3	4	5	6
7	8	9	10	11	12	13
14	15	16	17	18	19	20
21	22	23	24	25	26	27
28	29	30	31			

APRIL
S	M	T	W	T	F	S
				1	2	3
4	5	6	7	8	9	10
11	12	13	14	15	16	17
18	19	20	21	22	23	24
25	26	27	28	29	30	

MAY
S	M	T	W	T	F	S
						1
2	3	4	5	6	7	8
9	10	11	12	13	14	15
16	17	18	19	20	21	22
23	24	25	26	27	28	29
30	31					

JUNE
S	M	T	W	T	F	S
		1	2	3	4	5
6	7	8	9	10	11	12
13	14	15	16	17	18	19
20	21	22	23	24	25	26
27	28	29	30			

L

JULY

S	M	T	W	T	F	S
				1	2	3
4	5	6	7	8	9	10
11	12	13	14	15	16	17
18	19	20	21	22	23	24
25	26	27	28	29	30	31

AUGUST

S	M	T	W	T	F	S
1	2	3	4	5	6	7
8	9	10	11	12	13	14
15	16	17	18	19	20	21
22	23	24	25	26	27	28
29	30	31				

SEPTEMBER

S	M	T	W	T	F	S
			1	2	3	4
5	6	7	8	9	10	11
12	13	14	15	16	17	18
19	20	21	22	23	24	25
26	27	28	29	30		

OCTOBER

S	M	T	W	T	F	S
					1	2
3	4	5	6	7	8	9
10	11	12	13	14	15	16
17	18	19	20	21	22	23
24	25	26	27	28	29	30
31						

NOVEMBER

S	M	T	W	T	F	S
	1	2	3	4	5	6
7	8	9	10	11	12	13
14	15	16	17	18	19	20
21	22	23	24	25	26	27
28	29	30				

DECEMBER

S	M	T	W	T	F	S
			1	2	3	4
5	6	7	8	9	10	11
12	13	14	15	16	17	18
19	20	21	22	23	24	25
26	27	28	29	30	31	

M 1796 1808 1836 1864 1892
       1904 1932 1960 1988

JANUARY
S	M	T	W	T	F	S
					1	2
3	4	5	6	7	8	9
10	11	12	13	14	15	16
17	18	19	20	21	22	23
24	25	26	27	28	29	30
31						

FEBRUARY
S	M	T	W	T	F	S
	1	2	3	4	5	6
7	8	9	10	11	12	13
14	15	16	17	18	19	20
21	22	23	24	25	26	27
28	29					

MARCH
S	M	T	W	T	F	S
		1	2	3	4	5
6	7	8	9	10	11	12
13	14	15	16	17	18	19
20	21	22	23	24	25	26
27	28	29	30	31		

APRIL
S	M	T	W	T	F	S
					1	2
3	4	5	6	7	8	9
10	11	12	13	14	15	16
17	18	19	20	21	22	23
24	25	26	27	28	29	30

MAY
S	M	T	W	T	F	S
1	2	3	4	5	6	7
8	9	10	11	12	13	14
15	16	17	18	19	20	21
22	23	24	25	26	27	28
29	30	31				

JUNE
S	M	T	W	T	F	S
			1	2	3	4
5	6	7	8	9	10	11
12	13	14	15	16	17	18
19	20	21	22	23	24	25
26	27	28	29	30		

M

JULY
S	M	T	W	T	F	S
					1	2
3	4	5	6	7	8	9
10	11	12	13	14	15	16
17	18	19	20	21	22	23
24	25	26	27	28	29	30
31						

AUGUST
S	M	T	W	T	F	S
	1	2	3	4	5	6
7	8	9	10	11	12	13
14	15	16	17	18	19	20
21	22	23	24	25	26	27
28	29	30	31			

SEPTEMBER
S	M	T	W	T	F	S
				1	2	3
4	5	6	7	8	9	10
11	12	13	14	15	16	17
18	19	20	21	22	23	24
25	26	27	28	29	30	

OCTOBER
S	M	T	W	T	F	S
						1
2	3	4	5	6	7	8
9	10	11	12	13	14	15
16	17	18	19	20	21	22
23	24	25	26	27	28	29
30	31					

NOVEMBER
S	M	T	W	T	F	S
		1	2	3	4	5
6	7	8	9	10	11	12
13	14	15	16	17	18	19
20	21	22	23	24	25	26
27	28	29	30			

DECEMBER
S	M	T	W	T	F	S
				1	2	3
4	5	6	7	8	9	10
11	12	13	14	15	16	17
18	19	20	21	22	23	24
25	26	27	28	29	30	31

N
1780 1820 1848 1876
1916 1944 1972 2000

JANUARY
S	M	T	W	T	F	S
						1
2	3	4	5	6	7	8
9	10	11	12	13	14	15
16	17	18	19	20	21	22
23	24	25	26	27	28	29
30	31					

FEBRUARY
S	M	T	W	T	F	S
	1	2	3	4	5
6	7	8	9	10	11	12
13	14	15	16	17	18	19
20	21	22	23	24	25	26
27	28	29				

MARCH
S	M	T	W	T	F	S
			1	2	3	4
5	6	7	8	9	10	11
12	13	14	15	16	17	18
19	20	21	22	23	24	25
26	27	28	29	30	31	

APRIL
S	M	T	W	T	F	S
						1
2	3	4	5	6	7	8
9	10	11	12	13	14	15
16	17	18	19	20	21	22
23	24	25	26	27	28	29
30						

MAY
S	M	T	W	T	F	S
	1	2	3	4	5	6
7	8	9	10	11	12	13
14	15	16	17	18	19	20
21	22	23	24	25	26	27
28	29	30	31			

JUNE
S	M	T	W	T	F	S
				1	2	3
4	5	6	7	8	9	10
11	12	13	14	15	16	17
18	19	20	21	22	23	24
25	26	27	28	29	30	

N

JULY

S	M	T	W	T	F	S
						1
2	3	4	5	6	7	8
9	10	11	12	13	14	15
16	17	18	19	20	21	22
23	24	25	26	27	28	29
30	31					

AUGUST

S	M	T	W	T	F	S
		1	2	3	4	5
6	7	8	9	10	11	12
13	14	15	16	17	18	19
20	21	22	23	24	25	26
27	28	29	30	31		

SEPTEMBER

S	M	T	W	T	F	S
					1	2
3	4	5	6	7	8	9
10	11	12	13	14	15	16
17	18	19	20	21	22	23
24	25	26	27	28	29	30

OCTOBER

S	M	T	W	T	F	S
1	2	3	4	5	6	7
8	9	10	11	12	13	14
15	16	17	18	19	20	21
22	23	24	25	26	27	28
29	30	31				

NOVEMBER

S	M	T	W	T	F	S
			1	2	3	4
5	6	7	8	9	10	11
12	13	14	15	16	17	18
19	20	21	22	23	24	25
26	27	28	29	30		

DECEMBER

S	M	T	W	T	F	S
					1	2
3	4	5	6	7	8	9
10	11	12	13	14	15	16
17	18	19	20	21	22	23
24	25	26	27	28	29	30
31						

Time zones of the world
Some countries, including the UK, adopt Daylight
Saving Time (DST) in order to receive more daylight

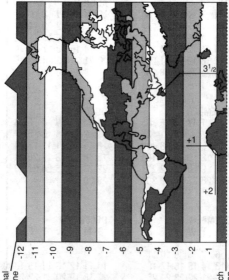

Time zones to the west of the Greenwich
Meridian are 'earlier' than Greenwich Mean
Time (GMT). For example, at 12 noon GMT it
is 7 am in New York (A).

in summer. Clocks are put forward 1 hour in spring and back 1 hour in autumn. The maps below do not reflect DST adjustments.

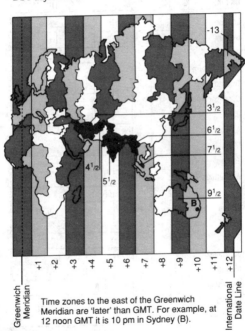

Time zones to the east of the Greenwich Meridian are 'later' than GMT. For example, at 12 noon GMT it is 10 pm in Sydney (B).

Office times The table shows the usual office hours (local time) in various cities compared with UK time.

UK time	Office hours
London	09.00
Sydney	09.00 – 12.00
Brussels	08.30 – 12.00
Rio de Janeiro	
Toronto	
Copenhagen	08.00
Paris	09.00 – 12.00
Athens	08.00 – 14.00
Milan	08.30 – 12.45
Tokyo	09.00 – 17.00
Amsterdam	08.30
Oslo	08.00
Lisbon	10.00 – 12.30
Dublin	09.30
Riyadh	08.00 – 13.00
Johannesburg	08.30
Madrid	09.30 – 13.30
Stockholm	08.30
Geneva	08.00 – 12.00
New York	
Frankfurt	08.00

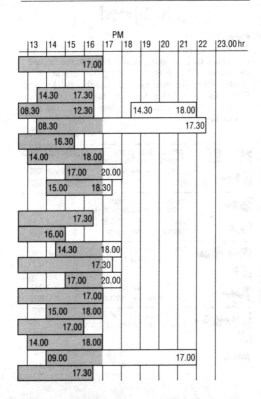

8: Speed

Formulas

Below are listed the multiplication/division factors for converting units of speed from imperial to metric, and vice versa; and, also, for converting from one unit to another within the same system. Note that two kinds of factors are given: quick, for an approximate conversion that can be made without a calculator; and accurate, for an exact conversion.

		Quick	**Accurate**
Miles per hour (mph)			
Kilometres per hour (km/h)			
mph ⟶ km/h		× 1.5	× 1.609
km/h ⟶ mph		÷ 1.5	× 0.621
Yards per minute (ypm)			
Metres per minute (m/min)			
ypm ⟶ m/min		× 1	× 1.094
m/min ⟶ ypm		÷ 1	× 0.914
Feet per minute (ft/min)			
Metres per minute (m/min)			
ft/min ⟶ m/min		× 3	× 3.281
m/min ⟶ ft/min		÷ 3	× 0.305
Inches per second (in/s)			
Centimetres per second (cm/s)			
in/s ⟶ cm/s		× 2.5	× 2.54
cm/s ⟶ in/s		÷ 2.5	× 0.394

	International knots (kn) Miles per hour (mph)	**Quick**	**Accurate**
kn ⟶ mph		× 1	× 1.151
mph ⟶ kn		÷ 1	× 0.869

	British knots (UK kn) International knots (kn)		
UK kn ⟶ kn		× 1	× 1.001
kn ⟶ UK kn		÷ 1	× 0.999

	International knots (kn) Kilometres per hour (km/h)		
kn ⟶ km/h		× 2	× 1.852
km/h ⟶ kn		÷ 2	× 0.540

	Miles per hour (mph) Feet per second (ft/s)		
mph ⟶ ft/s		× 1.5	× 1.467
ft/s ⟶ mph		÷ 1.5	× 0.682

	Kilometres per hour (km/h) Metres per second (m/s)		
km/h ⟶ m/s		× 3.5	× 3.599
m/s ⟶ km/h		÷ 3.5	× 0.278

Conversion tables

The tables below can be used to convert units of speed from one measuring system to another. The first group

Miles per hour to Kilometres per hour		Kilometres per hour to Miles per hour		Yards per minute to Metres per minute	
mph	km/h	km/h	mph	ypm	m/min
1	1.609	1	0.621	1	0.914
2	3.219	2	1.242	2	1.829
3	4.828	3	1.864	3	2.743
4	6.437	4	2.485	4	3.658
5	8.047	5	3.106	5	4.572
6	9.656	6	3.728	6	5.486
7	11.265	7	4.349	7	6.401
8	12.875	8	4.970	8	7.315
9	14.484	9	5.592	9	8.230
10	16.093	10	6.213	10	9.144
20	32.187	20	12.427	20	18.288
30	48.280	30	18.641	30	27.432
40	64.374	40	24.854	40	36.576
50	80.467	50	31.068	50	45.720
60	96.561	60	37.282	60	54.864
70	112.654	70	43.495	70	64.008
80	128.748	80	49.709	80	73.152
90	144.841	90	55.923	90	82.296
100	160.934	100	62.137	100	91.440

of tables converts imperial to metric, and vice versa.
The tables beginning on page 192 convert knots,
imperial and metric units.

Metres per minute to Yards per minute		Feet per minute to Metres per minute		Metres per minute to Feet per minute	
m/min	ypm	ft/min	m/min	m/min	ft/min
1	1.094	1	0.305	1	3.281
2	2.187	2	0.610	2	6.562
3	3.281	3	0.914	3	9.842
4	4.374	4	1.219	4	13.123
5	5.468	5	1.524	5	16.404
6	6.562	6	1.829	6	19.685
7	7.655	7	2.134	7	22.966
8	8.749	8	2.438	8	26.246
9	9.842	9	2.743	9	29.527
10	10.936	10	3.048	10	32.808
20	21.872	20	6.096	20	65.616
30	32.808	30	9.144	30	98.424
40	43.744	40	12.192	40	1.1.232
50	54.680	50	15.240	50	164.040
60	65.616	60	18.288	60	196.848
70	76.552	70	21.336	70	229.656
80	87.488	80	24.384	80	262.464
90	98.424	90	27.432	90	295.272
100	109.360	100	30.480	100	328.080

Imperial and metric units of speed (continued)

Inches per second to Centimetres per second		Centimetres per second to Inches per second		International knots to Miles per hour	
in/s	cm/s	cm/s	in/s	kn	mph
1	2.54	1	0.394	1	1.151
2	5.08	2	0.787	2	2.302
3	7.62	3	1.181	3	3.452
4	10.16	4	1.579	4	4.603
5	12.70	5	1.969	5	5.753
6	15.24	6	2.362	6	6.905
7	17.78	7	2.760	7	8.055
8	20.32	8	3.150	8	9.206
9	22.86	9	3.543	9	10.357
10	25.40	10	3.937	10	11.508
20	50.80	20	7.874	20	23.016
30	76.20	30	11.811	30	34.523
40	101.60	40	15.748	40	46.031
50	127.00	50	19.685	50	57.540
60	152.40	60	23.622	60	69.047
70	177.80	70	27.559	70	80.555
80	203.20	80	31.496	80	92.062
90	228.60	90	35.433	90	103.570
100	254.00	100	39.370	100	115.078

Miles per hour to International knots		UK knots to International knots		International knots to UK knots	
mph	kn	UK kn	kn	kn	UK kn
1	0.869	1	1.001	1	0.999
2	1.738	2	2.001	2	1.999
3	2.607	3	3.002	3	2.998
4	3.476	4	4.003	4	3.997
5	4.345	5	5.003	5	4.997
6	5.214	6	6.004	6	5.996
7	6.083	7	7.004	7	6.996
8	6.952	8	8.005	8	7.995
9	7.821	9	9.006	9	8.994
10	8.690	10	10.006	10	9.994
20	17.380	20	20.013	20	19.987
30	26.069	30	30.019	30	29.981
40	34.759	40	40.026	40	39.974
50	43.449	50	50.032	50	49.968
60	52.139	60	60.038	60	59.962
70	60.828	70	70.045	70	69.955
80	69.518	80	80.051	80	79.949
90	78.208	90	90.058	90	89.942
100	86.898	100	100.064	100	99.936

Imperial and metric units of speed (continued)

International knots to Kilometres per hour		Kilometres per hour to International knots		Miles per hour to Feet per second	
kn	km/h	km/h	kn	mph	ft/s
1	1.852	1	0.540	1	1.467
2	3.704	2	1.08	2	2.933
3	5.556	3	1.62	3	4.400
4	7.408	4	2.16	4	5.867
5	9.260	5	2.70	5	7.334
6	11.112	6	3.23	6	8.800
7	12.964	7	3.77	7	10.669
8	14.816	8	4.31	8	11.734
9	16.668	9	4.85	9	13.203
10	18.520	10	5.30	10	14.667
20	37.040	20	10.78	20	29.334
30	55.560	30	16.17	30	44.001
40	74.080	40	21.56	40	58.668
50	92.600	50	26.95	50	73.335
60	111.120	60	32.34	60	88.002
70	129.640	70	37.73	70	26.690
80	148.160	80	43.12	80	117.336
90	166.680	90	48.51	90	132.003
100	185.200	100	53.90	100	146.670

Feet per second to Miles per hour		Kilometres per hour to Metres per second		Metres per second to Kilometres per hour	
ft/s	mph	km/h	m/s	m/s	km/h
1	0.682	1	0.278	1	3.599
2	1.364	2	0.556	2	7.198
3	2.046	3	0.834	3	10.797
4	2.728	4	1.111	4	14.396
5	3.410	5	1.389	5	17.995
6	4.092	6	1.669	6	21.594
7	4.774	7	1.945	7	25.193
8	5.456	8	2.222	8	28.792
9	6.138	9	2.500	9	32.391
10	6.820	10	2.778	10	35.990
20	13.640	20	5.556	20	71.980
30	20.460	30	8.334	30	107.970
40	27.280	40	11.112	40	143.960
50	34.100	50	13.890	50	179.950
60	40.920	60	16.668	60	215.940
70	47.740	70	19.446	70	251.930
80	54.560	80	22.224	80	287.920
90	61.380	90	25.002	90	323.910
100	68.200	100	27.780	100	359.900

Wind speeds

Wind is the movement of air across the surface of the
Earth. Its direction is determined by a combination of
factors: the Earth's rotation, land features such as
mountains, and variations in the temperature and
pressure of the atmosphere.

Beaufort scale

Wind speed is measured using the internationally

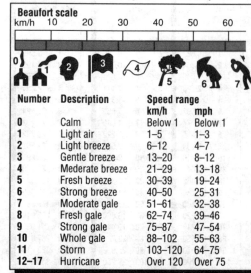

Number	Description	Speed range km/h	mph
0	Calm	Below 1	Below 1
1	Light air	1–5	1–3
2	Light breeze	6–12	4–7
3	Gentle breeze	13–20	8–12
4	Moderate breeze	21–29	13–18
5	Fresh breeze	30–39	19–24
6	Strong breeze	40–50	25–31
7	Moderate gale	51–61	32–38
8	Fresh gale	62–74	39–46
9	Strong gale	75–87	47–54
10	Whole gale	88–102	55–63
11	Storm	103–120	64–75
12–17	Hurricane	Over 120	Over 75

recognised Beaufort scale, named after the nineteenth-century British admiral, Sir Francis Beaufort.

Below are listed the Beaufort wind force numbers and the range of speeds to which they apply. The brief official descriptions show the variety of wind speeds that are measured, and examples of their physical manifestations are given to illustrate the strengths of

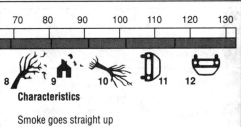

| 70 | 80 | 90 | 100 | 110 | 120 | 130 |

8   9   10   11   12

Characteristics

Smoke goes straight up
Smoke blows in wind
Wind felt on face
Extends a light flag
Raises dust and loose paper
Small trees begin to sway
Umbrellas hard to use
Inconvenient to walk into
Twigs broken off trees
Chimney pots and slates lost
Trees uprooted
Widespread damage
Extremely violent

9: Geometry

Polygons

Name of polygon	Number of sides	Each internal angle	Sum of internal angles
Triangle	3	60°	180°
Square	4	90°	360°
Pentagon	5	108°	540°
Hexagon	6	120°	720°
Heptagon	7	128.6°	900°
Octagon	8	135°	1080°
Nonagon	9	140°	1260°
Decagon	10	144°	1440°
Undecagon	11	147.3°	1620°
Dodecagon	12	150°	1800°

A Triangle
B Square
C Pentagon
D Hexagon
E Heptagon
F Octagon
G Nonagon
H Decagon
I Undecagon
J Dodecagon

Quadrilaterals

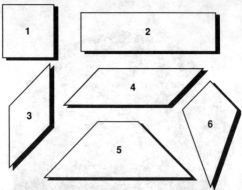

Quadrilaterals

A quadrilateral is a four-sided polygon.

1 Square		All the sides are the same length and all the angles are right angles.
2 Rectangle		Opposite sides are the same length and all the angles are right angles.
3 Rhombus		All the sides are the same length but none of the angles are right angles.
4 Parallelogram		Opposite sides are parallel to each other and of the same length.
5 Trapezium		One pair of the opposite sides is parallel.
6 Kite		Adjacent sides are the same length and the diagonals intersect at right angles.

Triangles

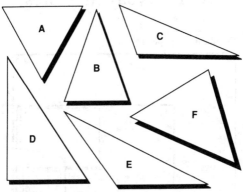

Triangles

A	Equilateral	All the sides are the same length and all the angles are equal.
B	Isosceles	Two sides are of the same length and two angles are of equal size.
C	Scalene	All the sides are of different length and all the angles are of different sizes.
D	Right angle	A triangle that contains one right angle.
E	Obtuse angle	A triangle that contains one obtuse angle.
F	Acute angle	A triangle with three acute angles.

10: Everyday measures

Standard UK paper sizes

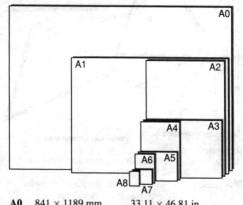

A0	841 × 1189 mm	33.11 × 46.81 in
A1	594 × 841 mm	23.39 × 33.11 in
A2	420 × 594 mm	16.54 × 23.39 in
A3	297 × 420 mm	11.69 × 16.54 in
A4	210 × 297 mm	8.27 × 11.69 in
A5	148 × 210 mm	5.83 × 8.27 in
A6	105 × 148 mm	4.13 × 5.83 in
A7	74 × 105 mm	2.91 × 4.13 in
A8	52 × 74 mm	2.05 × 2.91 in

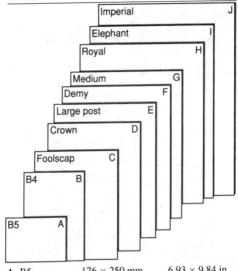

		mm	in
A	B5	176×250 mm	6.93×9.84 in
B	B4	250×353 mm	9.84×13.90 in
C	Foolscap	343×432 mm	13.50×17.00 in
D	Crown	381×508 mm	15.00×20.00 in
E	Large post	419×533 mm	16.50×21.00 in
F	Demy	445×572 mm	17.50×22.50 in
G	Medium	457×584 mm	18.00×23.00 in
H	Royal	508×635 mm	20.00×25.00 in
I	Elephant	508×686 mm	20.00×27.00 in
J	Imperial	559×762 mm	22.00×30.00 in

Envelope sizes and styles

Three of the most popular envelope styles are illustrated on the opposite page. There are many variations of each of these styles.

Below are illustrated the primary envelope sizes; the table opposite gives dimensions and the styles in which each is available.

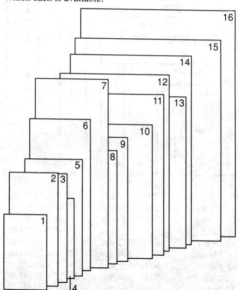

A Banker style
B Pocket style
C Window

Number	inches	mm	A	B	C
1	$3^1/_2$ x 6	89 x 152	•	•	•
2	4 x 9	102 x 229	•	•	•
3	$4^1/_4$ x $8^5/_8$	110 x 220	•	•	•
4	$4^1/_2$ x $6^3/_8$	114 x 162	•		•
5	$4^3/_4$ x $9^1/_4$	120 x 235	•	•	
6	5 x 12	127 x 305		•	
7	6 x 15	152 x 381		•	
8	$6^3/_8$ x 9	162 x 229	•	•	•
9	$6^7/_8$ x $9^7/_8$	175 x 250		•	
10	$8^1/_2$ x $10^5/_8$	216 x 270		•	
11	9 x $12^3/_4$	229 x 324		•	•
12	9 x 14	229 x 356		•	
13	10 x 12	254 x 305		•	
14	10 x 15	254 x 381		•	
15	12 x 16	305 x 406		•	
16	$12^3/_4$ x 18	324 x 457		•	

Book sizes

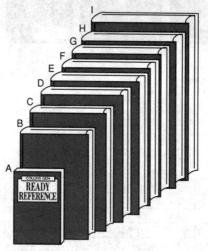

A	Collins Gem	117 × 79 mm	4.60 × 3.00 in
B	Foolscap octavo	170 × 110 mm	6.75 × 4.25 in
C	Crown octavo	190 × 125 mm	7.50 × 5.00 in
D	Large crown octavo	205 × 135 mm	8.00 × 5.25 in
E	Small demy octavo	215 × 145 mm	8.50 × 5.63 in
F	Demy octavo	220 × 145 mm	8.75 × 5.63 in
G	Medium octavo	230 × 145 mm	9.00 × 5.75 in
H	Small royal octavo	235 × 155 mm	9.25 × 6.13 in
I	Royal octavo	255 × 160 mm	10.00 × 6.25 in

Wine bottle shapes

Bordeaux

Burgundy; Moselle

Côtes de Provence

Alsace

Chianti

Hock

Clothing sizes

UK clothing sizes are equal to US sizes for some items, such as children's shoes; for others, the two vary slightly. Below are listed the European equivalents of UK and US clothing and shoe sizes. Remember also that sizes vary depending on the manufacturer.

Men's shoes

UK	USA	Europe
6½	7	39
7	7½	40
7½	8	41
8	8½	42
8½	9	43
9	9½	43
9½	10	44
10	10½	44
10½	11	45

Women's shoes

UK	USA	Europe
3½	5	36
4½	6	37
5½	7	38
6½	8	39
7½	9	40

Children's shoes

UK/USA	Europe
0	15
1	17
2	18
3	19
4	20
4½	21
5	22
6	23
7	24
8	25
8½	26
9	27
10	28
11	29
12	30
12½	31
13	32

Men's suits/overcoats

UK/USA	Europe
36	46
38	48
40	50
42	52
44	54
46	56

Men's shirts

UK/USA	Europe
12	30–31
12½	32
13	33
13½	34–35
14	36
14½	37
15	38
15½	39–40
16	41
16½	42
17	43
17½	44–45

Men's socks

UK/USA	Europe
9	38–39
10	39–40
10½	40–41
11	41–42
11½	42–43

Women's clothing

UK	USA	Europe
8	6	36
10	8	38
12	10	40
14	12	42
16	14	44
18	16	46
20	18	48
22	20	50
24	22	52

Children's clothing

UK	USA	Europe
16–18	2	40–45
20–22	4	50–55
24–26	6	60–65
28–30	7	70–75
32–34	8	80–85
36–38	9	90–95

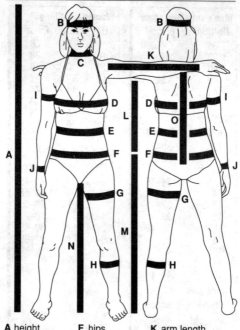

A height	**F** hips	**K** arm length
B head	**G** thigh	**L** armpit to hip
C neck	**H** calf	**M** outside leg
D chest/bust	**I** arm	**N** inside leg
E waist	**J** wrist	**O** back

Body measurements

The standard body measurements shown on the diagram on the opposite page are those needed for garment fitting.

Below are a few tips on taking some of these measurements.

Neck

Measure at the fullest part.

Chest/bust

Measure at the fullest part of the bust or chest and straight across the back.

Waist

Tie a string around the thinnest part of your body (the waist) and leave it there as a point of reference for other measurements.

Hips

There are two places to measure hips, depending on the garment: one is 2–4 in below the waist, at the top of the hipbones; the other is at the fullest part, usually 7–9 in below.

Arm

Measure at the fullest part, usually about 1 in below the armpit.

Arm length

Start at the shoulder bone and continue past the elbow to the wrist, with the arm slightly bent.

Back

Measure from the prominent bone in the back of the neck down the centre to the waist string.

Life expectancy

The table below shows life expectancy figures for selected countries. Age in years appears at the top of each bar.

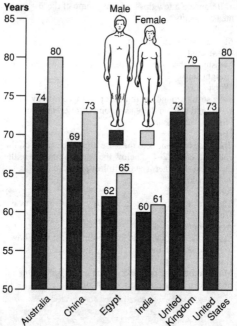

Years

Male Female

Country	Male	Female
Australia	74	80
China	69	73
Egypt	62	65
India	60	61
United Kingdom	73	79
United States	73	80

Average heights

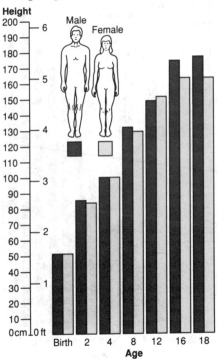

Average weights

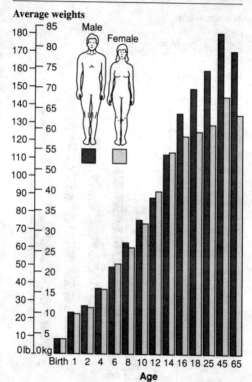

Laundry codes

Most garments contain a label giving laundering instructions, usually shown in terms of symbols, that tell you if any item is washable (or should be dry-cleaned) and how to wash it. The codes are listed below.

The table on the following pages lists the old and new codes, recommended temperatures (for machine- or hand-washing), and other machine settings, and the types of fabric that should be washed according to that code.

A Machine or hand wash
B Can be bleached
C Do not bleach
D Iron
E Do not iron

F Dry cleanable
G Do not dry clean
H Tumble dry
I Do not tumble dry

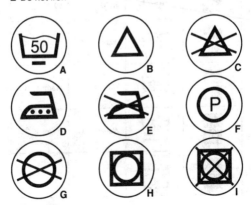

OLD	NEW	MACHINE WASH	HAND WASH
CODE		TEMPERATURE	
1 9 95 95	95	Very hot 95 °C to boil	Hand hot 50 °C or boil
2 3 60 60	60	Hot 60 °C	Hand hot 50 °C
4 50	50	Hand hot 50 °C	Hand hot 50 °C
5 40	40	Warm 40 °C	Warm 40 °C
6 40	40	Warm 40 °C	Warm 40 °C
7 40	40	Warm 40 °C	Warm 40 °C
8 30	30 30	Cool 30 °C	Cool 30 °C

AGITATION	RINSE	SPIN	FABRIC
Maximum	Normal	Normal	White cotton and linen with no special finish
Maximum	Normal	Normal	Cotton, linen, viscose, colour-fast with no special finish
Medium	Cold	Short spin or drip dry	Coloured nylon, polyester, cotton and viscose with special finish
Maximum	Normal	Normal	Cotton, linen, viscose, colour-fast to 40 °C
Minimum	Cold	Short spin	Acrylics, acetate and mixtures with wool
Minimum; do not rub	Normal	Normal; do not hand wring	Wool and wool mixtures
Minimum	Cold	Short spin; do not hand wring	Silk and printed acetate, not colour-fast at 40 °C

Gun gauge

A shotgun bore (diameter) is measured in millimetres, which are expressed in terms of gauge. Gauge was originally determined by the number of round lead balls – each the size of the shotgun bore – in a pound. For example, a 10-gauge shotgun was one that used balls that were 10 to the pound. The exception is the 410 bore, which is measured in inches: .410 in diameter, using 67.5 gauge. The most popular size today is the 12-gauge.

The table below shows gauge and equivalent bore size.

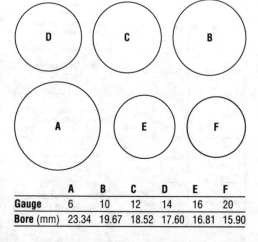

	A	B	C	D	E	F
Gauge	6	10	12	14	16	20
Bore (mm)	23.34	19.67	18.52	17.60	16.81	15.90

Horse measurements

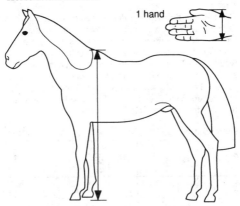

1 hand

The height of a horse or pony is measured to its withers (on the highest point on its back at the neck base), as shown above. Height is expressed in "hands high" (hh). One hand is 4 in (10 cm), the average width of a person's hand. Height is given to the nearest inch – a pony measuring 50 in (127 cm) is said to measure 12.2 hands. The table below shows recommended heights of ponies for young riders.

Pony's height (hh)	Child's age (years)
11–12	7–9
12–13	10–13
13–14.2	13–15
14.2–15.2	15–17

Odds in dice and cards
Dice

Odds in dice-throwing are determined by comparing favourable results with unfavourable. With one die, you have six possible results – one for each side of the die; with two die, you have 36 possible results. Some results – a 12 or a 2 – you have only one chance to achieve. Thus the odds against throwing a 12 or 2 are 35 to 1. For results with two possible combinations, the chances are 35 to 2, or 17 to 1. The table below shows the odds for each possible combination.

Combination	Chances	Combination
2	35–1	12
3	17–1	11
4	11–1	10
5	8.5–1	9
6	7–1	8
7	5–1	

Poker

Odds in poker are figured against a total number of possible combinations of 2 598 960. Thus, the odds of getting a royal flush (4 possible combinations) are 2 598 960 to 4, or 649 739 to 1.

Hand	Chances
royal flush	649 739 to 1
straight flush	72 192 to 1
four of a kind	4164 to 1
full house	693 to 1
flush	508 to 1
straight	254 to 1
three of a kind	46 to 1
two pair	20 to 1
one pair	2.4 to 1
nil	2 to 1

Blackjack

There are a possible 1326 combinations in blackjack; the odds of reaching 21 with two cards from a 52-card deck (64 possible combinations) are thus 1326 to 64, or 21 to 1.

Two-card total	Chances
21	21 to 1
20	9 to 1
19	16.5 to 1
18	15 to 1
17	14 to 1
16	15 to 1
15	14 to 1
14	13 to 1
13	11 to 1

11: Astronomy

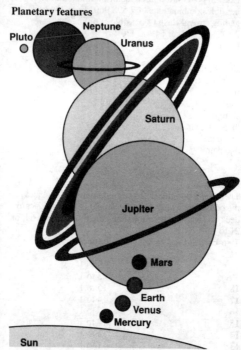

Planetary features

Pluto

Neptune

Uranus

Saturn

Jupiter

Mars

Earth

Venus

Mercury

Sun

Diameter at equator

Planet	km	mi
Mercury	4878	2926.8
Venus	12 104	7262.4
Earth	12 756	7653.6
Mars	6795	4077.0
Jupiter	142 800	85 680.0
Saturn	120 000	72 000.0
Uranus	50 800	30 480.0
Neptune	48 500	29 100.0
Pluto	3000	1800.0

Rotation period

Mercury	58 days 15 hr
Venus	243 days
Earth	23 hr 56 min
Mars	24 hr 37 min
Jupiter	9 hr 50 min
Saturn	10 hr 14 min
Uranus	16 hr 10 min
Neptune	18 hr 26 min
Pluto	6 days 9 hr

Average surface temperatures

Solid surface		Cloud surface	
Mercury {	350 °C (day)	Jupiter	−150 °C
	−170 °C (night)	Saturn	−180 °C
Venus	480 °C	Uranus	−210 °C
Earth	22 °C	Neptune	−220 °C
Mars	−23 °C	Pluto	−230 °C

Planetary distances

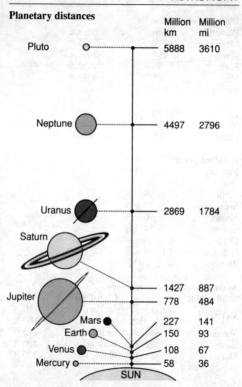

	Million km	Million mi
Pluto	5888	3610
Neptune	4497	2796
Uranus	2869	1784
Saturn	1427	887
Jupiter	778	484
Mars	227	141
Earth	150	93
Venus	108	67
Mercury	58	36

Mean distance from the Sun

Planet	km	mi
Mercury	58 000 000	36 000 000
Venus	108 000 000	67 000 000
Earth	150 000 000	93 000 000
Mars	227 000 000	141 000 000
Jupiter	778 000 000	484 000 000
Saturn	1 427 000 000	887 000 000
Uranus	2 869 000 000	1 784 000 000
Neptune	4 497 000 000	2 796 000 000
Pluto	5 888 000 000	3 661 000 000

Closest distance to the Earth

Planet	km	mi
Mercury	80 800 000	50 000 000
Venus	40 400 000	25 000 000
Mars	56 800 000	35 000 000
Jupiter	591 000 000	367 000 000
Saturn	1 198 000 000	744 000 000
Uranus	2 585 000 000	1 607 000 000
Pluto*	4 297 000 000	2 670 000 000
Neptune	4 308 000 000	2 678 000 000

*Between 1979 and 1999 Pluto will be closer to the Earth than Neptune because of the unusual shape of its orbit.

The solar system – Orbits and rotation

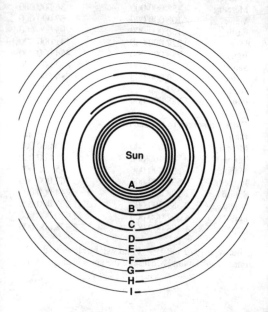

Sidereal period
Sidereal period is the time it takes a planet to orbit the
Sun. Planets' orbital speeds vary, as does their distance
from the Sun, so these periods are different for each
planet. The diagram shows how far each planet travels
in its orbit during the time it takes the Earth to
complete one orbit (approximately 1 year).

		Sidereal period	Average orbital speed
A	Mercury	88.0 days	47.9 km/s
B	Venus	224.7 days	35.0 km/s
C	Earth	365.3 days	29.8 km/s
D	Mars	687.0 days	24.1 km/s
E	Jupiter	11.86 years	13.1 km/s
F	Saturn	29.46 years	9.6 km/s
G	Uranus	84.01 years	6.8 km/s
H	Neptune	164.8 years	5.4 km/s
I	Pluto	247.7 years	4.7 km/s

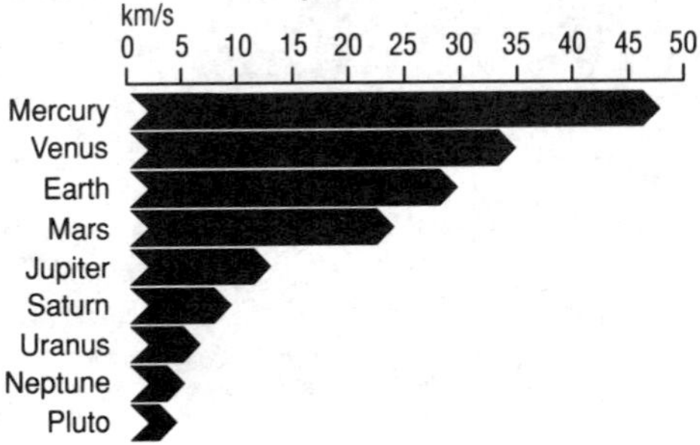

Light years

The table below lists standard abbreviations and equivalents for the units used in measuring astronomical distances. These are very large units and are related to the Earth's orbit.

A light year (ly) is the distance light travels – at its speed of 299 792.458 km/s – through space over a tropical year.

An astronomical unit (au) is the mean distance between the Earth and the Sun.

A parsec (pc) is the distance at which a baseline of 1 au in length subtends an angle of 1 second.

1 au = 149 600 000 km = 93 000 000 mi
1 ly = 9 460 500 000 000 km = 5 878 000 000 000 mi
1 pc = 30 857 200 000 000 km = 19 174 000 000 000 mi
1 ly = 63 240 au
1 pc = 206 265 au = 3.262 ly

Planetary data

	Mercury	Venus	Earth
Mean distance from Sun	0.39 au	0.72 au	1.00 au
Distance at perihelion	0.31 au	0.72 au	0.98 au
Distance at aphelion	0.47 au	0.73 au	1.02 au
Closest distance to Earth	0.54 au	0.27 au	
Average orbital speed	47.9 km/s	35.0 km/s	29.8 km/s
Rotation period	58 days 15 hr	243 days	23 hr 56 min
Sidereal period	88 days	224.7 days	365.3 days
Diameter at equator	4878 km	12 104 km	12 756 km
Mass (Earth's mass=1)	0.06	0.82	1
Surface temperature	350 °C (day) −170 °C (night)	480 °C	22 °C
Gravity (Earth's gravity = 1)	0.38	0.88	1
Density (density of water = 1)	5.5	5.25	5.517
Number of satellites known	0	0	1
Number of rings known	0	0	0
Main gases in atmosphere	no atmosphere	Carbon dioxide	Nitrogen, oxygen

Planetary data (continued)

	Mars	Jupiter
Mean distance from Sun	1.52 au	5.20 au
Distance at perihelion	1.38 au	4.95 au
Distance at aphelion	1.67 au	5.46 au
Closest distance to Earth	0.38 au	3.95 au
Average orbital speed	24.1 km/s	13.1 km/s
Rotation period	24 hr 37 min	9 hr 50 min
Sidereal period	687 days	11.86 years
Diameter at equator	6795 km	142 800 km
Mass (Earth's mass=1)	0.11	317.9
Surface temperature	−23 °C	−150 °C
Gravity (Earth's gravity = 1)	0.38	2.64
Density (density of water = 1)	3.94	1.33
Number of satellites known	2	16
Number of rings known	0	1
Main gases in atmosphere	Carbon dioxide	Hydrogen, helium

Saturn	Uranus	Neptune	Pluto
9.54 au	19.18 au	30.06 au	39.36 au
9.01 au	18.28 au	29.80 au	29.58 au
10.07 au	20.09 au	30.32 au	49.14 au
8.01au	17.28 au	28.80 au	28.72 au
9.6 km/s	6.8 km/s	5.4 km/s	4.7 km/s
10 hr 14 min	16 hr 10 min	18 hr 26 min	6 days 9 hr
29.46 years	84.01 years	164.8 years	247.7 years
120 000 km	50 800 km	48 500 km	3000 km
95.2	14.6	17.2	0.002–0.003
−180 °C	−210 °C	−220 °C	−230 °C
1.15	1.17	1.2	not known
0.71	1.7	1.77	not known
19	5	2	1
1000+	9	0	0
Hydrogen, helium	Hydrogen, helium, methane	Hydrogen, helium, methane	Methane

12: Earth

Earth's interior

A Crust (under oceans) 6 km (4 mi) deep; made of basalt (a type of rock). Crust (continental): average 35 km (22 mi) deep; made of granite

B Mantle 2900 km (1800 mi) deep; probably containing peridotite (a heavy, dark rock), dunite (olivine rock) and ecologite (a dense form of basalt)

C Outer core 2000 km (1240 mi) deep; probably liquid iron with some dissolved sulphur and silicon

D Inner core 1370 km (850 mi) deep; probably solid iron

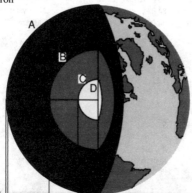

21	2935	4935	6291 km from Earth's crust
13	1823	3065	3906 mi from Earth's crust

Atmospheric layers and depths of the Earth

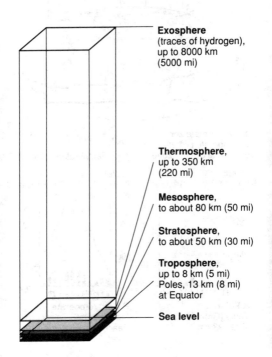

Exosphere
(traces of hydrogen),
up to 8000 km
(5000 mi)

Thermosphere,
up to 350 km
(220 mi)

Mesosphere,
to about 80 km (50 mi)

Stratosphere,
to about 50 km (30 mi)

Troposphere,
up to 8 km (5 mi)
Poles, 13 km (8 mi)
at Equator

Sea level

World climates

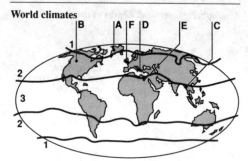

1 Polar climate zone
2 Temperate climate zone
3 Tropical climate zone

 = Rainfall (mm)

 = Temperature (°C)

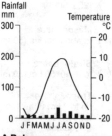

A Polar
Thule (Greenland)
Total: 93mm

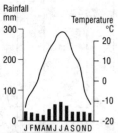

**B Cold temperate
(continental)**
Peace river (Canada)
Total: 376mm

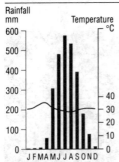

C Tropical (monsoon)
Rangoon (Burma)
Total: 2620mm

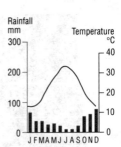

D Warm temperate
Athens (Greece)
Total: 402mm

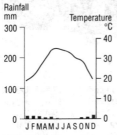

E Tropical (desert)
Cairo (Egypt)
Total: 25mm

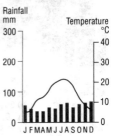

F Cool temperate (marine)
London (UK)
Total: 593mm

Continents

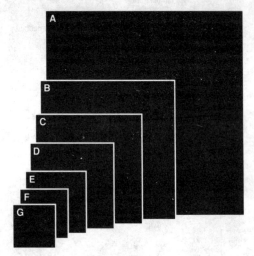

A Asia	44 250 000 km²	17 085 000 mi²
B Africa	30 264 000 km²	11 685 000 mi²
C N. America	24 398 000 km²	9 420 000 mi²
D S. America	17 793 000 km²	6 870 000 mi²
E Antarctica	13 209 000 km²	5 100 000 mi²
F Europe	9 907 000 km²	3 825 000 mi²
G Australia	8 534 000 km²	3 295 000 mi²

Largest countries

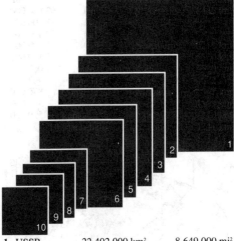

1	USSR	22 402 000 km²	8 649 000 mi²
2	Canada	9 976 000 km²	3 852 000 mi²
3	China	9 561 000 km²	3 692 000 mi²
4	USA	9 520 000 km²	3 676 000 mi²
5	Brazil	8 512 000 km²	3 286 000 mi²
6	Australia	7 682 000 km²	2 966 000 mi²
7	India	3 288 000 km²	1 269 000 mi²
8	Argentina	2 777 000 km²	1 072 000 mi²
9	Sudan	2 506 000 km²	968 000 mi²
10	Zaïre	2 345 000 km²	905 000 mi²

Oceans and seas

		km²	mi²
1	Pacific Ocean	165 242 000	63 800 000
2	Atlantic Ocean	82 362 000	31 800 000
3	Indian Ocean	73 556 000	28 400 000
4	Arctic Ocean	13 986 000	5 400 000
5	South China Sea	2 975 000	1 149 000
6	Caribbean Sea	2 753 000	1 063 000
7	Mediterranean Sea	2 505 000	967 000
8	Bering Sea	2 269 000	876 000
9	Gulf of Mexico	1 544 000	596 000
10	Sea of Okhotsk	1 528 000	590 000

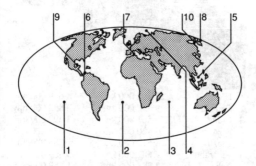

Largest islands

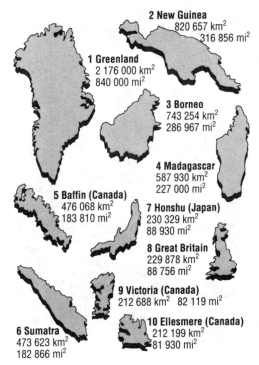

2 New Guinea
820 657 km^2
316 856 mi^2

1 Greenland
2 176 000 km^2
840 000 mi^2

3 Borneo
743 254 km^2
286 967 mi^2

4 Madagascar
587 930 km^2
227 000 mi^2

5 Baffin (Canada)
476 068 km^2
183 810 mi^2

7 Honshu (Japan)
230 329 km^2
88 930 mi^2

8 Great Britain
229 878 km^2
88 756 mi^2

9 Victoria (Canada)
212 688 km^2 82 119 mi^2

10 Ellesmere (Canada)
212 199 km^2
81 930 mi^2

6 Sumatra
473 623 km^2
182 866 mi^2

Volcanoes and mountains

Highest volcanoes

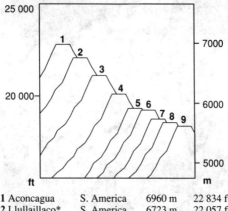

	1 Aconcagua	S. America	6960 m	22 834 ft
	2 Llullaillaco*	S. America	6723 m	22 057 ft
	3 Chimborazo	S. America	6267 m	20 560 ft
	4 McKinley	N. America	6194 m	20 320 ft
	5 Cotopaxi†	S. America	5896 m	19 344 ft
	6 Kilimanjaro	Africa	5895 m	19 340 ft
	7 Antisana	S. America	5704 m	18 713 ft
	8 Citlaltepetl	S. America	5700 m	18 700 ft
	9 Elbrus	Europe	5633 m	18 480 ft

* Quiescent   †Active

Highest mountains

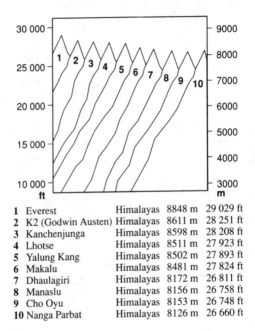

1	Everest	Himalayas	8848 m	29 029 ft
2	K2 (Godwin Austen)	Himalayas	8611 m	28 251 ft
3	Kanchenjunga	Himalayas	8598 m	28 208 ft
4	Lhotse	Himalayas	8511 m	27 923 ft
5	Yalung Kang	Himalayas	8502 m	27 893 ft
6	Makalu	Himalayas	8481 m	27 824 ft
7	Dhaulagiri	Himalayas	8172 m	26 811 ft
8	Manaslu	Himalayas	8156 m	26 758 ft
9	Cho Oyu	Himalayas	8153 m	26 748 ft
10	Nanga Parbat	Himalayas	8126 m	26 660 ft

Highest mountain in each continent
When reading the figure, note the discontinuity
between 5000 ft and 15 000 ft, and 2000 m and 4000 m.

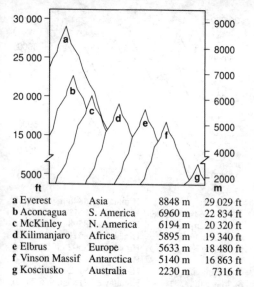

a Everest	Asia	8848 m	29 029 ft
b Aconcagua	S. America	6960 m	22 834 ft
c McKinley	N. America	6194 m	20 320 ft
d Kilimanjaro	Africa	5895 m	19 340 ft
e Elbrus	Europe	5633 m	18 480 ft
f Vinson Massif	Antarctica	5140 m	16 863 ft
g Kosciusko	Australia	2230 m	7316 ft

Highest mountain in selected countries

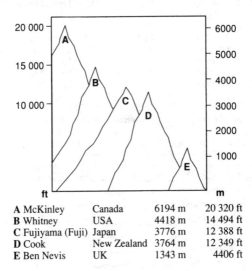

A McKinley	Canada	6194 m	20 320 ft
B Whitney	USA	4418 m	14 494 ft
C Fujiyama (Fuji)	Japan	3776 m	12 388 ft
D Cook	New Zealand	3764 m	12 349 ft
E Ben Nevis	UK	1343 m	4406 ft

Longest rivers

1	Nile	Africa	6650 km	4132 mi
2	Amazon	S. America	6437 km	4000 mi
3	Mississippi-Missouri-Red Rock	N. America	6212 km	3860 mi
4	Ob-Irtysh	Asia	5570 km	3461 mi
5	Yangtze (Chang)	Asia	5520 km	3430 mi
6	Huang He	Asia	4672 km	2903 mi
7	Congo (Zaire)	Africa	4667 km	2900 mi
8	Amur	Asia	4509 km	2802 mi
9	Lena	Asia	4270 km	2653 mi
10	Mackenzie	N. America	4241 km	2635 mi

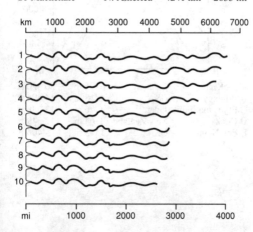

Longest in its continent

A Africa	Nile	6650 km	4132 mi
B S. America	Amazon	6437 km	4000 mi
C N. America	Mississippi- Missouri- Red Rock	6212 km	3860 mi
D Asia	Ob-Irtysh	5570 km	3461 mi
E Europe	Volga	3690 km	2293 mi
F Australia	Murray	3219 km	2000 mi

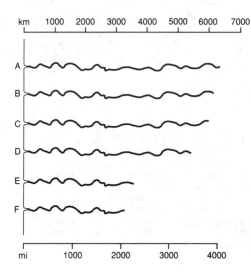

Largest lakes

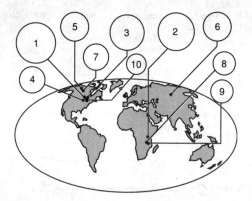

1	Superior	82·400 km²	31 800 mi²
2	Victoria	69 500 km²	26 800 mi²
3	Huron	59 600 km²	23 000 mi²
4	Michigan	58 000 km²	22 400 mi²
5	Great Bear	31 800 km²	12 300 mi²
6	Baykal	31 500 km²	12 200 mi²
7	Great Slave	28 400 km²	11 000 mi²
8	Tanganyika	28 400 km²	11 000 mi²
9	Malawi	28 200 km²	10 900 mi²
10	Erie	25 700 km²	9 900 mi²

Largest waterfalls

1 Angel, Venezuela
979 m (3212 ft)

2 Tugela, S. Africa
948 m (3110 ft)

3 Utigörd, Norway
800 m (2625 ft)

4 Mongefossen, Norway
774 m (2540 ft)

5 Yosemite, USA
739 m (2425 ft)

6 Østre Mardøla Foss,
Norway
657 m (2154 ft)

7 Tyssestrengane, Norway
646 m (2120 ft)

8 Kukenaom, Venezuela
610 m (2000 ft)

9 Sutherland, N. Zealand
580 m (1904 ft)

10 Kjellfossen, Norway
561 m (1841 ft)

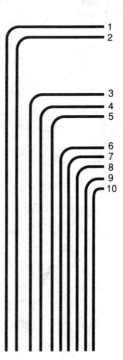

Largest deserts

A	Sahara	8 397 000 km²	3 242 000 mi²
B	Australian	1 549 000 km²	598 000 mi²
C	Arabian	1 300 000 km²	502 000 mi²
D	Gobi	1 039 000 km²	401 000 mi²
E	Kalahari	521 000 km²	201 000 mi²

F Turkestan	360 000 km²	139 000 mi²
G Takla Makan	321 000 km²	124 000 mi²
H Sonoran	311 000 km²	120 000 mi²
I Namib	311 000 km²	120 000 mi²
J Thar	259 000 km²	100 000 mi²

Deepest caves

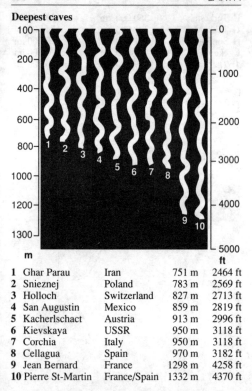

1	Ghar Parau	Iran	751 m	2464 ft
2	Snieznej	Poland	783 m	2569 ft
3	Holloch	Switzerland	827 m	2713 ft
4	San Augustin	Mexico	859 m	2819 ft
5	Kacherlschact	Austria	913 m	2996 ft
6	Kievskaya	USSR	950 m	3118 ft
7	Corchia	Italy	950 m	3118 ft
8	Cellagua	Spain	970 m	3182 ft
9	Jean Bernard	France	1298 m	4258 ft
10	Pierre St-Martin	France/Spain	1332 m	4370 ft

Capitals of the world
Africa
ALGERIA Algiers
ANGOLA Luanda
BENIN Porto-Novo
BOTSWANA Gaborone
BURKINA FASO
  Ouagadougou
BURUNDI Bujumbura
CAMEROON Yaoundé
CAPE VERDE Praia
CENTRAL AFRICAN
REPUBLIC Bangui
CHAD N'Djamena
COMOROS Moroni
CONGO Brazzaville
DJIBOUTI Djibouti
EGYPT Cairo
EQUATORIAL GUINEA
  Malabo
ERITREA Asmara
ETHIOPIA Addis Ababa
GABON Libreville
GAMBIA Banjul
GHANA Accra
GUINEA Conakry
GUINEA-BISSAU
  Bissau
IVORY COAST
(COTE D'IVOIRE)
  Yamoussoukro/Abidjan
KENYA Nairobi

LESOTHO Maseru
LIBERIA Monrovia
LIBYA Tripoli
MADAGASCAR
  Antananarivo
MALAWI Lilongwe
MALI Bamako
MAURITANIA
  Nouakchott
MAURITIUS Port Louis
MOROCCO Rabat
MOZAMBIQUE Maputo
NAMIBIA Windhoek
NIGER Niamey
NIGERIA Abuja
RWANDA Kigali
SÃO TOMÉ AND
PRINCÍPE São Tomé
SENEGAL Dakar
SEYCHELLES Victoria
SIERRA LEONE Freetown
SOMALIA Mogadishu
SOUTH AFRICA
  Cape Town/ Pretoria
SUDAN Khartoum
SWAZILAND Mbabane
TANZANIA Dodoma
TOGO Lomé
TUNISIA Tunis
UGANDA Kampala
ZAÏRE Kinshasa
ZAMBIA Lusaka

ZIMBABWE Harare

Asia and Middle East
AFGHANISTAN Kabul
BAHRAIN Manama
BANGLADESH Dhaka
BHUTAN Thimphu
BRUNEI Bandar Seri
  Begawan
CAMBODIA
  Phnom Penh
CHINA Beijing
INDIA New Delhi
INDONESIA Jakarta
IRAN Tehran
IRAQ Baghdad
ISRAEL Jerusalem
JAPAN Tokyo
JORDAN Amman
KOREA, NORTH
  Pyongyang
KOREA, SOUTH Seoul
KUWAIT Kuwait City
LAOS Vientiane
LEBANON Beirut
MALAYSIA
  Kuala Lumpur
MALDIVES Malé
MONGOLIA Ulan Bator
MYANMAR(Burma)
  Yangon (Rangoon)
NEPAL Kathmandu

OMAN Muscat
PAKISTAN Islamabad
PHILIPPINES Manila
QATAR Doha
SAUDI ARABIA Riyadh
SINGAPORE Singapore
SRI LANKA Colombo
SYRIA Damascus
THAILAND Bangkok
TURKEY Ankara
UNITED ARAB
  EMIRATES Abu Dhabi
VIETNAM Hanoi
YEMEN Sana'a

Europe
ALBANIA Tirana
ANDORRA
  Andorra la Vella
AUSTRIA Vienna
BELGIUM Brussels
BULGARIA Sofia
CYPRUS Nicosia
CZECHOSLOVAKIA
  Prague
DENMARK Copenhagen
ESTONIA Tallinn
FINLAND Helsinki
FRANCE Paris
GERMANY Berlin
GREECE Athens
HUNGARY Budapest

ICELAND Reykjavík
IRELAND (Eire) Dublin
ITALY Rome
LATVIA Riga
LIECHTENSTEIN Vaduz
LITHUANIA Vilnius
LUXEMBOURG
  Luxembourg
MALTA Valletta
MONACO Monaco-Ville
NETHERLANDS
  The Hague/Amsterdam
NORWAY Oslo
POLAND Warsaw
PORTUGAL Lisbon
ROMANIA Bucharest
RUSSIA Moscow
SAN MARINO
  San Marino
SPAIN Madrid
SWEDEN Stockholm
SWITZERLAND Bern
UNITED KINGDOM
  London
VATICAN CITY
  Vatican city
YUGOSLAVIA Belgrade

Australasia
AUSTRALIA Canberra
FIJI Suva
KIRIBATI Tarawa

MARSHALL ISLANDS
  Dalap-Uliga-Darrit
MICRONESIA
  Kolonia
NAURU Yaren
NEW ZEALAND
  Wellington
PALAU Koror
PAPUA NEW GUINEA
  Port Moresby
SOLOMON ISLANDS
  Honiara
TONGA Nuku'alofa
TUVALU Funafuti
VANUATU Port-Vila
WESTERN SAMOA Apia

South America
ARGENTINA Buenos
  Aires
BOLIVIA La Paz/Sucre
BRAZIL Brasília
CHILE Santiago
COLOMBIA Bogotá
ECUADOR Quito
FRENCH GUIANA
  Cayenne
GUYANA Georgetown
PARAGUAY Asunción
PERU Lima
SURINAME Paramaribo
URUGUAY Montevideo

VENEZUELA Caracas

North and Central America

ANTIGUA AND BARBUDA St John's
BAHAMAS Nassau
BARBADOS Bridgetown
BELIZE Belmopan
CANADA Ottawa
COSTA RICA San José
CUBA Havana
DOMINICA Roseau
DOMINICAN REPUBLIC Santo Domingo
EL SALVADOR San Salvador
GREENLAND Nuuk
GRENADA St George's
GUATEMALA Guatemala City
HAITI Port-au-Prince
HONDURAS Tegucigalpa
JAMAICA Kingston
MEXICO Mexico City
NICARAGUA Managua
PANAMA Panama City
ST LUCIA Castries
ST CHRISTOPHER AND NEVIS Basseterre
ST VINCENT AND THE GRENADINES Kingstown
TRINADAD AND TOBAGO Port of Spain
UNITED STATES OF AMERICA Washington DC